APPEARANCE
IS
EVERYTHING

APPEARANCE IS EVERYTHING

The Hidden Truth Regarding Your Appearance & Appearance Discrimination

Steve Jeffes

Sterling House
PUBLISHER
Pittsburgh, PA

ISBN 1-156315-088-3

Trade Paperback
© Copyright 1998 Steve Jeffes
All rights reserved
First Printing—1998
Library of Congress #: 98-85255

Request for information should be addressed to:

Sterling House Publisher
The Sterling Building
440 Friday Road
Department T-101
Pittsburgh, PA 15209

Cover design & Typesetting: Drawing Board Studios

Printed in the United States of America

DEDICATION

This book is dedicated to anyone who has been discriminated against or has been effected by the obsession with appearance.

This book is also dedicated to my wife, Annette who has supported me through many of life's trials and tribulations, including the development of this book.

CREDITS

*I wish to thank the following people and organizations
for making this book possible:*

Al Haddad for his encouragement and support
Steve Newton for his supreme editing expertise
Tom Cash for his encouragement and suggestion of research materials
Carrier-UTC Corporation for their support via the Diversity Council
The Syracuse Updowntowners for their constant encouragement and input
Sabrina Paris from Springer-Verlag for incredible support in obtaining permissions
*All contributors and friends at the Lockheed-Martin Corporation and
General Electric Corporations*

and most of all

*My Parents,
Marie and Millard
and my wife
Annette*

TABLE OF CONTENTS

INTRODUCTION

What do other people think of **you** based on your appearance? How do these people treat you as a result of what they think of your appearance? Have you ever wondered what affect your appearance has on your ability to not only attract mates, to land a job, get promoted, make friends, obtain wealth, and interact with others in society? Every day people are making value judgments based solely on your appearance. Every time you go to the mall, to work, to a beach, to a picnic, to a party, people are making value judgments (right or wrong) about your worth, your intelligence, your ability to parent, and even your ability to contribute to society based solely on your appearance. In many instances these value judgments based on appearance are wrong and often discriminatory.

Much effort has been spent on the general topic of discrimination. Discrimination based on race, sex, age, disability, and national origin all receive much public attention and awareness. Appearance discrimination is another form of discrimination which is becoming pervasive throughout society, yet is rarely mentioned. Appearance discrimination is rampant today as notions of "thin is in" and "body beautiful" are promoted. Eating disorders are at epidemic proportions as people try to "fit" the thinner beauty ideal. In a more sound-bite, time-limited world of the 90's, we are making judgments more and more based on a person's appearance. We do not have the luxury of time to "get to know" the true person based on the personality, sense of humor, contributions, etc.. Our judgments of people and their worth are more and more being driven primarily by their appearance. We are truly and dangerously becoming an appearance driven society.

For example, have you ever noticed that very attractive people in society seem to be afforded far more opportunities and better treatment than are less attractive people? Did you know that it has been proven that **attractive people**:

1. Are afforded the opportunity to earn more money (12% more)
2. Have disproportionately more opportunities to date, marry, and produce offspring
3. Are assumed to have greater intelligence, capability, and personality

Did you also know that **unattractive people**:

1. Are disproportionately abused as children
2. Are assumed by society to be less intelligent, capable, and less likely to succeed in life
3. Are excluded from being hired and promoted in certain industries and occupations

Your next question is probably what can be done to change this discriminatory situation and change the way we are viewed by others. You are probably wondering if there is something that you can do to improve your situation and improve you appearance posture? The answers to these and many other questions are contained in this book along with many valuable insights on how you can:

1. Take our appearance test to determine your appearance quotient (AQ) and determine where you fall in the bell-curve of societal appearance distribution. Are you beautiful (top 2%), very attractive (15%), average (66% of society), unattractive (15%), or very unattractive (bottom 2%). Find out what this "score" means for you and your outlook on life.
2. Become successful and wealthy regardless of your appearance
3. Avoid being discriminated based on your appearance during you career including:
    a. During a lay-off situation
    b. When you are up for a promotion
    c. When being interviewed for a job
    d. During the course of performing your duties
    e. Recognizing an appearance discriminatory boss or work environment
4. Effectively recognize and combat appearance discrimination directed at you and your family
5. Recognize if your lover or spouse is appearance (in)compatible
6. Increase your odds of dating, marrying, and making new friends regardless of your appearance
7. Teach your children the proper attitudes toward their appearance as well as the appearance of others
8. Recognize problems regarding your children's appearance and their treatment by other children
9. Avoid becoming beauty obsessed and isolated in society
10. Learn how to effectively improve your appearance and how others change their opinion of you based on this improvement
11. How to change forever the way you look at yourself, spouse, family, friends, and others based on amazing appearance-based revelations and concepts

The 45 RULES GOVERNING APPEARANCE DISCRIMINATION

Also included are 45 appearance rules which can lead to a better understanding of the dynamics associated with appearance discrimniation and result in a happier, more successful life for those who realize their powerful implications. This book can change your life by radically influencing the way you look at other people and how they look at you. The insights from this book may astound you and will most surely challenge your present views.

1. ATTRACTIVE PERSONS are generally ASSUMED to have higher levels of intelligence, motivation, education, and overall capability.

2. ATTRACTIVE PERSONS are generally provided greater opportunities for obtaining wealth, career growth, and marrying successfully than an unattractive person of similar intelligence, education, and motivation.

3. UNATTRACTIVE PERSONS are generally ASSUMED to have lower than average intelligence, education, and motivation.

4. UNATTRACTIVE PERSONS are generally provided fewer opportunities for obtaining wealth, career growth, and marrying successfully than an attractive person of similar intelligence, education, and motivation.

5. Over eighty percent (80%) of all MEN AND WOMEN at one time or another are seeking to attain a mate in the top 20% of attractiveness.

6. MEN & WOMEN alike use appearance or attractiveness as the FIRST discriminator to determine whether to socialize, date, and marry. After a minimum acceptable level of appearance has been met THEN come factors such as sense of humor, kindness, honesty, wealth, power, etc.

7. MEN will engage in short-term relationships with persons of lower appearance with the sole purpose of obtaining sex. WOMEN will typically not engage is this type of short-term behavior due to their desire to make love, not merely have sex.

8. WOMEN in general tend to place a heavier emphasis on factors such as personality, status, sincerity, honesty, kindness, and openness than appearance and do so more than men.

9. INSECURE OLDER WOMEN who lacked a strong father figure during their childhood tend to select older, powerful, dominant men rather than very attractive men. These less secure women feel safer, secure and compensated for their lack of identity through their powerful/dominant mate.

10. The YOUNGER a person is, the more he/she will rely on attractiveness as the key factor in determining whether they will form a relationship with someone.

11. INSECURE OLDER MEN & WOMEN continue to rely on attractiveness as the key factor in determining whether they will form a relationship with a person of the opposite sex.

12. INSECURE MEN seek women who are inferior in intellect and stature, yet who are more attractive. In this manner, men can stand out as the dominate partner and appear, in a microcosm, to be a person of accomplishment (good provider with an attractive mate).

13. SECURE MEN & WOMEN tend to shift from appearance to other factors such as life goal compatibility, ability to get along, and intellectual factors in mate selection.

14. SUCCESSFUL RELATIONSHIPS (friends, marriage, dating) are those that are generally formed between two people of extremely close appearance (female height usually shorter than male height by no more than 10%, weight similar for given frame, similar hair color, etc..)

15. COUPLES tend to talk, act, and more incredibly APPEAR more alike over time.

16. Persons of SIMILAR ATTRACTIVENESS tend to socialize exclusively with persons of similar attractiveness. Very attractive(category 1's), moderately attractive(2's), average(3's), and less than average(4/5's) persons socialize with other persons within their attractiveness categories.

17. The more an organization or position deals with the public, the greater the likelihood that an attractive person will be hired, promoted, and receive higher compensation over an unattractive person.

18. Attractive persons have been found to be more effective in the art of persuasion (i.e. Sales, marketing, public relations, t.v.commercials, etc.)

19. Facially attractive people are expected to possess socially and organizationally desirable personality traits (warm, sensitive, etc.).

20. Attractive persons are assumed to possess greater ability in a job than unattractive persons.

21. The less mature, more autonomous, or less educated a manager is within an organization, the more likely he/she will hire, fire, promote and make assignments based on a factors other than ability (i.e. Appearance, friendship, sex, race, etc.).

22. The more a manager is consumed by their own appearance, the more likely they will be to be concerned with, and discriminate against, yours.

23. You should act, dress, and appear like the person in the position you desire to obtain without compromising your integrity or ethical standards

24. Persons of greater means (wealthier) generally have greater opportunity to attain an attractive appearance since they have easier access to appearance enhancement equipment, facilities, experts, and services. Persons of lesser means have fewer opportunities to improve their appearance and must apply extra effort and personal conviction to overcome the lack of access to appearance enhancing equipment, facilities, experts, and services.

25. Since attractive persons are generally treated more favorably in life, they tend to develop high levels of self-esteem and self-confidence. These high levels of self-esteem and self-confidence provide greater potential to succeed in life.

26. Since unattractive persons are generally treated less favorably in life, they tend to evolve low levels of self-esteem and self-confidence. These low levels of self-esteem and self-confidence detract from their chance to succeed in life.

27. Attractive persons are generally provided greater opportunities to socialize and make friends than unattractive persons of similar capabilities. This pro-

vides the attractive greater opportunities to build networks in order to succeed in life, business, and other endeavors.

28. Very beautiful women who wear diamond rings will almost always have larger diamonds (1 carat+) than women who are less attractive and also wear diamond rings.

29. Persons who are attractive have a distinct advantage in obtaining success, wealth, power and advances in life over equally qualified, yet less attractive persons. These person have a higher rating of "a" in the life success formula and may be more successful, depending on their goals or tasks being attempted.

30. The greater the levels of affluence in a given area, the more likely the appearance standard will be higher.

31. Areas whose economies rely on influence industries (legal, sales, management, marketing, brokering, public relations, financial management) tend to maximize the importance of a persons appearance.

32. Areas which encourage or maintain higher levels of affluence often encourage and maintain higher levels of personal appearance.

33. Areas whose economy relies on labor intensive and outdoor oriented industries tend to minimize the importance of a person's appearance.

34. Areas which are relatively isolated from media influences (t.v., radio, magazines, newspapers, etc.) often maintain lower appearance standards than areas designated as media mecca.

35. The older a person becomes, the less likely they are to make assumptions about a person based on their appearance provided they have: 1) had exposure to persons who are contradictory to the standard paradigm that attractive persons are inherently valuable and unattractive persons are inherently not valued 2) they are intelligent enough to understand the lesson from the contradictory paradigm under #1 above.

36. People whose success relies on appearance will tend to value and be sensitive to their own appearance, as well as value others with similar appearance standards. The statement in this instance is simply "what brings success to me is good, what is good for me (attractive appearance) must then be good for others. The same is true for intelligence, knowledge, physical strength, etc. This is one of the reasons we tend to gravitate towards others with similar "values".

37. The more we are educated as children to be aware of our own appearance, the more aware and sensitive we will be about other people's appearance.

38. Just as in adult life, we must recognize that we have limits and cannot be someone we are not. Likewise, we must teach our children to recognize their strengths and value their differences.

39. An overweight person is ascribed many negative personality traits and thoughts compared to a non-overweight person. An overweight person will receive far less favorable treatment than a non-overweight person.

40. Dress in such a way that you are not made to feel uncomfortable or inferior by those around you or those you unexpectedly come in contact with, including those who directly affect your livelihood or chance for success

41. People will first judge you by your appearance, then by your personality if time and opportunity permits. The longer your exposure to a another person, the greater your chance of being judged on personality traits versus appearance factors.

42. Persons who are very attractive, yet possess very negative personality characteristics (i.e. Lacking in personality, mean, manipulative, pushy, etc.) are likely to experience the same type of negative treatment by society as is experienced by some unattractive persons.

43. The more a person is exposed to media portraying atypical and highly beautiful persons, the more likely a person will consciously or unconsciously become self-conscious, disappointed, angry, or withdrawn over their own appearance if they do not appear similarly attractive.

44. 1) beauty attracts attention and is pleasant to view 2) since beauty is pleasant to view, we logically want to prolong our exposure and contact with the beauty source (person, flower, lake, etc.). 3) since we tend to notice and lock visually onto the beauty source, we are more likely to focus on the message or product being brought forth by this beauty source. The message or product is therefore mentally associated with something beautiful and pleasant. 4) the beauty source therefore is more effective in selling and influencing than someone unattractive that would be either not noticed or purposely ignored. 5) beauty, therefore sells more effectively and is sought out by the media disproportionately more than those who are average or unattractive in appearance.

45. People who are both unattractive and externally motivated are more likely to succumb to the effects of lowered self-confidence, self-esteem, and motivation due to criticism and rejection by others than internally motivated people.

RULE PROVED IN CHAPTER	APPEARANCE RULES
Chapter 1	1-4
Chapter 2	5-16
Chapter 3	17-23
Chapter 4	24-29
Chapter 5	30-36
Chapter 6	37-38
Chapter 7	39-42
Chapter 8	43-45

CHAPTER
1

DETERMINE YOUR
APPEARANCE QUOTIENT (AQ)!

Every time someone views you for the first time, they reach a quick, sub-conscience conclusion about your appearance. Perhaps someone next to you in the book store, supermarket, or at work is making that judgment right now. Ever wondered the type of thinking that goes on to draw such a conclusion? How can one make such a quick, sub-conscious decision? What factors make up this judgment? What ramifications does this judgment have on you, your treatment, and your chances for success and happiness? This chapter is devoted to assist you by breaking down the process of how appearance decisions are made into two simple steps.

Extensive research, observation, and experiments led me to conclude that the world's population is divided into five distinct categories of attractiveness. They are:

Beautiful   (Category 1)   Attractive   (Category 2)
Average   (Category 3)   Unattractive   (Category 4)
Very Unattractive   (Category 5)

The percentage of persons in each category was noted at many large public gatherings over 8 years. The five distinct categories were a direct result of distinctly different comments made by persons observed at these events. These appearance-related comments and the corresponding derived categories are:

"That person is gorgeous or beautiful"   (Category 1)

"That person is (very) attractive"   (Category 2)

"That person is good looking or average";
"There is nothing wrong with him/her"   (Category 3)

"That person is not very attractive";
"That person doesn't appeal to me";
"That person isn't very nice looking"   (Category 4)

"That person looks awful/ ugly/horrible";
"I feel badly for that person";
"That person is homely"   (Category 5)

1

APPEARANCE IS EVERYTHING

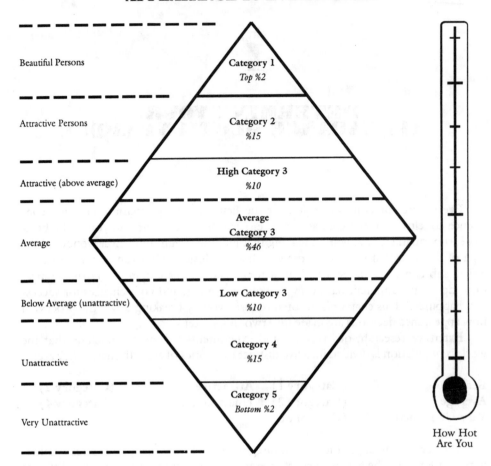

Societal Appearance Distribution & Categorization
Chart 1

Each category represents a percentage of the total population. Chart 1 shows that categories 1 and 5 represent the smallest percentage population at 2% each, with category 1 representing the "most attractive" and category 5 representing the "least attractive" persons. Category 2 represents 15% of the population as "attractive" while category 4 represent another 15% as "unattractive." Chart 1 research indicates that the appearance categories are symmetrical on either side of the "average" category meaning there are as many people above average as there are below average in appearance. Think of a pyramid sitting alongside a mirror that displays the pyramid standing upright as upside down. The effect would be as shown in chart 1. The negative or opposite image of a "beautiful" person is a "very unattractive" person as the opposite image of "attractive" is "unattractive." There is no opposite of the "average" person since this represents the base of the pyramid where only a single image appears on either side. The opposite categories are significant in that they represent how each category is treated by society. High(top of pyramid) categories receive most favorable treatment while low (bottom of pyramid) categories receive mostly unfavorable treatment. High appearance categories have greater chances for career growth, relationships, and overall success while lower categories are generally given much lower chances for life's fruits.

We see opposite the attractive appearance image, where better treatment and opportunity for success exists, is the mirror image of "unattractive", where people have less chances offered for success and fair treatment. Also notice from chart 1 that nearly half of society falls within the "average" category. In other words, while much attention is played to the extremes, the majority of the population is just average, unobtrusive people whose appearance receives neither abnormal positive or negative comment. The instruments of society would, through numerous magazines, TV ads, and daily bombardment of appearance improvement messages, have us believe that society is almost entirely comprised of category 1's & 2's, and that we are "missing the boat" by being anything but one of these (actually rare) individuals. No wonder people turn to psychotherapy in record numbers while the average weight of Miss America has dropped 30% over the last 30 years!

The different life-styles and class distinctions between these appearance categories are profound, yet largely ignored. Everyone falls into an appearance category, yet the process for determining this category goes on quietly in a person's subconscious and is rarely discussed, particularly if the category is less than positive (i.e., category 4 or category 5). The following exercise will not only help you determine your category, but also detail the brief mental exercise we all go through to categorize (& discriminate) each other's appearance. The point totals for each question category were based on observations and questionnaires from many areas of the country. This survey took into *account a study conducted by Terry and Davis in 1976, asked persons in a study to rate other persons based on photographs "dissected into the separate facial components, viz., mouth, eyes, hair, nose, and facial structure, which were pasted onto similar file cards and coded on the reverse side to permit later matching." The study "resulted in the following order of importance for the components; mouth (r=.53),eyes(r=.44), structure(r=.43), hair (r=.34), and nose(r=.31)."*

For example, the first question concerns weight. Our society, in general, discriminates against overweight persons of all categories while only the thinnest people are ridiculed for being too thin. The point system reflects this societal preference for thinner versus overweight persons. The remaining questions were engineered based on this concept of Preference of the Majority (of society).

To determine your category you must first determine your Appearance Quotient (AQ) score from the following 15 questions. Next, utilize the score to determine where you fall within the described categories (1-5) below. The categorization of appearance in one of the five categories allows a one-dimensional view of how your appearance affects your life. Other factors (variables) such as intelligence, education, and age are considered constant for the purpose of this exercise. Later in chapter 6, we'll look at the effects that intelligence, education, and age have on appearance discrimination. The questions are quite frank so please be honest with yourself or have a close personal friend, mate, or relative rate each category for you. A perfect score would be 500, putting you on top of the "beautiful" category (Category 1).

APPEARANCE IS EVERYTHING

Determine YOUR Appearance Quotient (AQ)

Question	*Points*
1. Weight	
A. Correct weight for your height	50
B. Overweight by 10% or less	20
C. Overweight by 20% or less	5
D. Overweight by more than 20%	0
E. Underweight by 10% or less	40
F. Underweight by 20% or less	30
G. Underweight by 30% or less	15
H. Overweight by more than 30%	0

_____Points

2. Facial Features

A. Muscular face w/high cheek bones (men)	50
B. Petite, cute w/high cheek bones (women)	40
C. Thin facial features (w/o high check bones and not petite)	30
D. Pudgy facial features	10
E. Scarring, marks, very flabby/bony	0

_____Points

3. Physique

A. Muscular, fit, small buttocks, muscular or shapely chest	50
B. Average build	25
C. Flabby or bony appearance	0

_____Points

4. Eyes

A. Large eyes with deep color/sparkle	40
B. Average eyes	20
C. Sunken eyes or bulging eyes	0

_____Points

5. Hair

A. Full of body, deep color, attractive styling	40
B. Average Hair	20
C. Frizzy, brittle, or unkempt	10
D. Bald or Balding	0

_____Points

6. Sexual Presence

A. Sexy, sultry, *ASSUMED* to be able to provide
uninhibited sexual performance levels (women)   40
B. Sensual, firm but kind, strong (men)   40
C. Average or questionable sexual
performance assumed   20
D. Boring, shy, inhibited, robotic sexual
performance assumed   0

_____Points

7. Dress

A. Well dressed w/latest, expensive fashions
(very clean & stylish)   40
B. Well dressed with average style/quality clothes   20
C. Raggedy or worn clothes   10
D. Dirty & ragged clothes   0

_____Points

8. Nose

A. Medium or small (proportional to face)   30
B. Average to large   10
C. Very large or crooked   0

_____Points

9. Mouth/Lips

A. Medium-sized mouth & lips   30
B. Large or small lips   15
C. Non-existent or extremely large lips   0

_____Points

10. Teeth

A. Straight/very white   30
B. Slightly crooked/off-white (average)   15
C. Very crooked/yellowed/missing   0

_____Points

11. Ears
A. Small—close to head   20
B. Medium size, slightly protruding from head   10
C. Large, very protruding, malformed ears   0

_____ Points

12. Body Proportions
A. Arms, legs, torso, head in proportion   20
B. Arms, legs, torso, head *slightly* disproportionate   10
C. Arms, legs, torso, head *very* disproportionate   0

_____ Points

13. Grooming
A. Perfectly groomed hair and nails at all times   20
B. Average grooming most of the time (neat)   10
C. Unkempt, dirty most of the time   0

_____ Points

14. Posture/Poise
A. Walks with confidence/sits straight   20
B. Walks with normal/slow gait, varied sitting positions   10
C. Struts, walks erratically, slouches when sitting   0

_____ Points

15. Cleanliness
A. Very clean, excellent personal hygiene   20
B. Average cleanliness   10
C. Dirty, smelly, grimy   0

_____ Points

TOTAL QUIZ POINTS   _____

POINTS	AQ	YOU ARE
400-500	1	"BEAUTIFUL"
300-399	2	"VERY ATTRACTIVE"
200-299	3	"AVERAGE"
100-199	4	"UNATTRACTIVE"
000-099	5	"VERY UNATTRACTIVE"

CATEGORY 1—BEAUTIFUL PERSONS (top 2% of attractiveness scale)
Note that while category 1 is the highest level of attractiveness it comprises just 2% of the total population. Category 1's are characterized as follows:

* You have a strikingly **beautiful appearance**. You are very pleasant to look at—you often elicit a smile from others.
* You attained a score of 400-500 on the AQ score card.
* You have a flawless body (weight proportionate to frame, good muscle tone, hair full of body & character, slightly muscular build).
* You have flawless facial features including high cheek bones, unblemished skin, and radiant face.
* You have large, bright eyes (dark brown, blue, or green).
* Your teeth are very straight and white.
* You dress impeccably with expensive clothes and accessories.
* You are well groomed and always appear with hair in place, nails manicured, face shaven.
* Your personal hygiene is impeccable.
* You have the ability to appear in society's highest appearance circles (men—cover of GQ, women—Cosmopolitan).
* Most persons make it a point to look at you when you enter a room and you usually elicit stares or strong glances from members of the opposite sex.
* Your profession tends to associate you with being attractive (model, actor/actress, marketing rep./Exec., Sales, public relations).
* Persons secretly fantasize about being with you, of dating or marrying you, or of having their mate appear as attractive as you.
* You have many friends, literally hundreds of dating relationships, opportunities to marry, and numerous job offers.
* Many people long to be seen in your presence and strive to be your friend.
* You tend to socialize with other very attractive persons/couples.
* You tend to shun persons of lower appearance categories (particularly categories 3-5).
* You tend to be superficial and used to getting your way.
* You tend to live in warm climates and larger cities/towns.
* People treat you with respect and possibly assume you have high levels of motivation, education, and intelligence.

CATEGORY 2—ATTRACTIVE PERSONS (15% of attractiveness scale)
Category 2 individuals are deemed attractive persons by society yet still comprise only 15% of the population. Category 2's are characterized as follows:

* You are generally classified as an **ATTRACTIVE** person by others.
* You attained a score of 300-399 on the AQ questionnaire.
* You have nice bodily and/or facial features.
* About 20-50% of persons take notice of your presence when you enter a room(friends excluded).

* You have many friends, opportunities to date/marry, and career options.
* You tend to socialize with other attractive persons/couples.
* You tend to shun persons of lower appearance categories (particularly categories 4 & 5).
* You are sometimes superficial and usually get your own way.

CATEGORY 3—AVERAGE PERSONS (66% of the overall scale)

Category 3 comprises the majority and are deemed AVERAGE attractive persons by society. Category 3's (probably you, and definitely me) are characterized as follows:

* You are usually classified as **AVERAGE** in attractiveness by other persons.
* You obtained a score of 200-299 of the AQ scorecard. If you obtained a 250—congratulations, you're exactly average!
* Your body features and/or facial features are comfortable to view.
* Probably not more than 20% of persons take more than a cursory look when you enter a room (friends excluded)
* You'd like to improve to category 1/2 if given the chance.
* You have an average number of average friends, opportunities to date/marry, and career opportunities (far less, however, than category 1's or 2's).
* You generally have to work harder than category 1's & 2's in making friends, obtaining career opportunities, and wealth.
* You tend to socialize with other average attractive persons/couples as well as lower category 2's and upper category 4's.

CATEGORY 4—UNATTRACTIVE PERSONS (15% of attractiveness scale)

The next lowest level of attractiveness are deemed UNATTRACTIVE by society and characterized as follows:

* You are usually classified as **UNATTRACTIVE** by others.
* You attained an AQ of 100-199 on the appearance category questionnaire.
* Few people make an effort to look at you when you enter a room (friends excluded).
* You have few friends, opportunities to date/marry, and career opportunities, unless your personality and/or intelligence are above average.
* You tend to socialize primarily with other unattractive persons/couples.
* You tend to be shunned by persons of higher appearance categories (particularly categories 1 & 2).
* You are occasionally angered by situations where you are limited in opportunity over higher appearance category persons.
* You tend to live in smaller towns and rural areas where you can remain isolated.
* Your occupation is usually unrelated to appearance and where interaction with other persons is limited.
* You tend to avoid public places and personal interaction.
* Meetings with others often elicits a negative or sour facial response.

Determine Your Appearance Quotient

CATEGORY 5—VERY UNATTRACTIVE (bottom 2%)
Only the bottom 2% of the population are deemed **VERY UNATTRACTIVE** persons by society. Category 5's are characterized as follows:

* You are usually classified as a **VERY UNATTRACTIVE** person by others.
* You obtained a score of 0-99 on the AQ questionnaire.
* You tend to have very few friends, opportunities to date/marry, and career opportunities unless your personality and/or intelligence is remarkable.
* You tend to not socialize.
* You tend to be shunned by most persons of higher appearance categories (categories 1-4).
* You are sometimes a very angry person due to life's limitations relative to all other categories.
* You tend to live in smaller towns and rural areas where you can remain isolated.
* Your occupation is most likely unrelated to appearance where interaction with other persons is not required or highly limited.
* You tend to avoid public places and personal interaction.
* Meetings with others may elicit a strongly negative facial expression and/or personal response.

The five categories are merely guidelines to determine where YOU stand in terms of appearance and the comparable treatment *YOU MAY* receive. Many other factors affect they way you're treated such as personality, accomplishments, intelligence, age, and the type of persons with which you socialize. This exercise illustrates how appearance may lead to unfair treatment by others BEFORE they really know anything about you and illustrates that discrimination occurs for appearance just as for race, creed, color, etc.. Note yourself the favorable treatment afforded attractive persons relative to those falling in the less attractive categories (4's & 5's). Four appearance rules come into play in this instance. Rules #1 and 2 directly apply to biases toward an ATTRACTIVE person based on appearance. First, we'll look at the rules relating to attractive persons and provide graphic proofs for each. Answer the questions in the proofs honestly and think of examples where the proofs may have been true at sometime in your life. If (in the unlikely event) you disagree, I congratulate you, for you are a person who does not discriminate based upon appearance. I think you'll find, however, that at one point or another in your life, YOU HAVE DISCRIMINATED based on appearance.

Appearance rule #1:

Attractive persons are generally ASSUMED to have higher levels of intelligence, motivation, education and overall capability.

The proofs for rule #1 are:

1. Would your *first impression* of an extremely well dressed, beautiful or gorgeous person with impeccable grooming be that they are a derelict, lazy, unintelligent,

uneducated? Most likely your first impression would be the opposite, and be very favorable. Why do you think that persons who have committed the most heinous crimes are coached (by attorneys) to get a haircut, wear a freshly pressed suit, appear clean shaven, and even coached in proper speech usage?

2. Have you ever *assumed* that because a person is well dressed and very attractive that they are somewhat accomplished and probably well educated or highly intelligent? You probably rationalize that, since they are well dressed and very attractive, they must have the means to wear such nice clothes and maintain a nice appearance, hence must be educated, intelligent, hold a good job, etc..

3. What would be your *first impression* if your son or daughter brought home an extremely attractive person (of the opposite sex) for the first time? You'd probably have a very pleasant reaction. "Wow, my son/daughter's going out with a very attractive person! How many times have you heard a parent actually brag about their son or daughter's attractive boyfriend, girlfriend, fiancee, or spouse? I personally have lost count.

Appearance rule #2:

Attractive persons are generally provided greater opportunities for obtaining wealth, career growth, and marrying successfully than unattractive persons of similar intelligence, education, and motivation.

The proofs for rule #2 are:

1. Would it sway your decision if you were to interview two qualified persons for a job where one applicant was far more attractive and better dressed better than the other? Your decision would definitely be swayed toward the more attractive candidate if that person had to deal with the public!

2. Given the choice of anyone in the world to marry, if you weren't already married or involved with someone, would you select a homely person or someone very attractive (TV/movie star, model, etc.)?

3. Most upper level corporate positions require much greater interaction with the public than lower level ones. If you owned a company, would you not want your most visible positions (Chief Executive Officer, Chief Operating Officer, Public Relations director, etc. to be held by attractive persons in order to best represent your company? You likely would not select a very unattractive person! In this instance the saying **"put your company's best face forward"** has greater meaning!

4. Given that you agree with selection of the most attractive person available for your company in #3 above, who then in corporate America has the greatest chance for obtaining wealth? Again, the attractive person!

Rules 3 & 4 are the opposite of rules 1 & 2 in that they describe the treatment afforded the unattractive person in terms of opportunities provided in life by society.

Appearance Rule #3:

Unattractive persons are generally ASSUMED to have lower than average intelligence, education, and motivation (converse of rule #1).

The proofs for rule #3 are:

1. Would your *first impression* of a poorly dressed, very unattractive person with average grooming be that they are highly educated, highly accomplished, and are earning lots of money? Most likely your first impression would be just the opposite (very unfavorable.) Just think of the way you first reacted to the last very unattractive person you met.

2. Have you ever automatically *assumed* that, because a person is poorly dressed and very unattractive, they are lazy, unaccomplished and probably uneducated or unintelligent? You probably rationalize that, since they are poorly dressed and very unattractive, they must not have the means to wear good clothes and maintain a nice appearance, hence they must be uneducated, unintelligent, have an unskilled job, etc..

3. What would be your *first impression* if your son or daughter brought home an extremely unattractive person as their date for the first time? You would probably have a negative, even unpleasant reaction. "Oh no—my son/daughter's going out with a very unattractive person! What will my grandchildren look like?! He/she can surely do better than that!"

Appearance Rule #4:

Unattractive persons are generally provided fewer opportunities for obtaining wealth, career growth, and marrying successfully than attractive persons of similar intelligence, education, and motivation (converse of rule #2).

The proofs for rule #4 are:

1. How many times in the past have you sought out an unattractive person to date? Have you ever heard of anyone purposely seeking an unattractive person to date or marry? Not likely. How many times have you or others you know sought an unattractive mate? Does it not then follow that unattractive persons have far fewer opportunities to date, marry, etc.?

2. Given that most people seek attractive persons to date and marry, what other ramifications does this have for the unattractive person? Would you likely hire an unat-

tractive person to run your store or company if they had to deal with the public? Would you promote an unattractive person or an attractive person to CEO, COO, Public Relations director, etc.? Or, would you select an equally capable attractive person, provided one was available? If so, would it not be true that unattractive persons are generally provided fewer opportunities for obtaining wealth, and career growth?

3. How many times have you seen unattractive persons in Marketing, Television (news anchors, weather persons, commercials, soap opera stars, etc.), Real Estate, Public Relations, Receptionist, Host/Hostess, etc.? Is this coincidence or accident? Why are unattractive persons, with similar capabilities, not usually found in these positions? More importantly, what is being said about the attractive persons in these positions? Do people listen to/watch them more? Why wouldn't an unattractive person be just as effective? What is the underlying psychology? What was your reaction to the last (and rare) commercial featuring an overweight/unattractive person? It was probably not received as favorably as those with beautiful women/men.

4. When was the last time you saw a cosmetics or fashion commercial or newspaper ad featuring an unattractive person? Isn't this billion dollar bombardment saying in essence, "IT IS NOT OK OR NORMAL TO BE UNATTRACTIVE?" The media leads us to believe these beautiful models, actors/actresses, personalities, etc. are the ideals which the rest of society must attempt to become. If it were OK to be average or unattractive, then why would we need to buy all those appearance enhancing products? If you don't look and appear as these models, you must work at getting to be attractive and desirable. We're being taught each and every day that UNATTRACTIVE = UNDESIRABLE. Everyone aspires to be attractive and avoid those less fortunate and unattractive.

CHAPTER 1 SUMMARY

A. Appearance discrimination is rampant and affects everyone.
B. People use a subconscious process similar to the AQ quiz to determine how attractive YOU are.
C. Very unattractive or very attractive people are rare in society.
D. Average persons comprise over 50% of all persons in society.
E. Attractive persons are generally afforded greater opportunities in life than are unattractive persons.
F. *People should resist the temptation to discriminate based solely on a person's appearance.*

CHAPTER
2

YOUR APPEARANCE QUOTIENT DETERMINES YOUR PROSPECTS FOR FRIENDSHIP, ROMANCE, LOVE, AND MARRIAGE

Have you ever wondered what affect your appearance has on your ability to form relationships with persons of the opposite sex, to make friends with certain groups of people, and even to marry happily ever after? The fact is, once you understand how others view your appearance (as discussed in Chapter 1) and apply this understanding to the Rules of Appearance which govern relationships in this chapter, you will more likely succeed in forming meaningful relationships. Here we take a close look at the dynamics of how your appearance affects your every attempt to form sexual relationships, make friends, love the right person, and marry successfully.

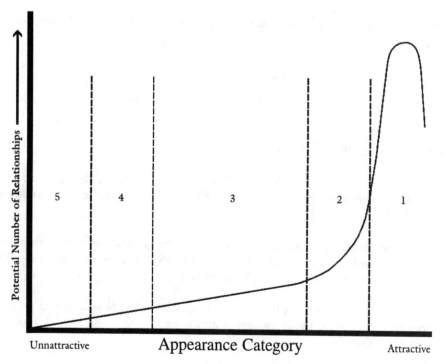

Relationship Between Appearance & Potential Number of Relationships
chart 2

APPEARANCE IS EVERYTHING

A. HOW YOUR APPEARANCE AFFECTS THE NUMBER OF RELATION-SHIPS YOU'LL FORM

Most people would agree that attractive persons have greater opportunity to date, form sexual relationships, and marry than do less attractive persons. However, a rather large disparity exists between opportunities (to form relationships) provided to the most attractive persons versus the opportunities provided persons in the lower attractiveness categories. The opportunities provided to category 1 (Beautiful) persons is almost unlimited, if they capitalize on them. Category 2 (Attractive) persons also have many opportunities to form relationships and have little problem finding dates, forming sexual and loving relationships, and marrying. Chart 2 shows the opportunities presented for categories 3-5 fall far below that of categories 1 & 2. The force of nature is at work here as many people attempt to "maximize" the attractiveness of their potential mate for any of the following reasons:

1) Secure an attractive mate to produce attractive, healthy offspring;
2) Obtain an attractive mate which will reflect on themselves as being attractive or accomplished;
3) Infatuation with another person's attractiveness (sometimes confused with true love);
4) Simply being with an attractive person may seem more important than compatibility.

Appearance Rule #5

"Over 80% of all people at one time or another seek to attain a mate in the top 20% of attractiveness."

The proofs for fule #5 are:

1) How many men or women have you known that continue to turn their head at passing very attractive men or women LONG AFTER they are steadily dating, engaged, or even married?

2) How many times have you seen two persons of the same sex out together, where one is far more attractive than the other, and only the more attractive person is pursuing, or being pursued, sexually or conversationally?

3) How many times have you been with a large number of people, where persons from both sexes seem to center their attention and conversation toward the more attractive person(s) in the room?

4) How many times have you met someone of the opposite sex who seemed only mildly interested in talking with you, but then literally "came alive" when another more attractive person of your sex entered the picture?

5) Extremely attractive persons have been known and documented to have hundreds, even (believe it or not) thousands of dates during their dating years. How does that compare to your numbers? If you are like most people (average), probably much fewer.

REAL LIFE EXAMPLE OF RULE #5:

Seven college friends and I attended a social function to enjoy a night away from our studies. Our group ranged (in attractiveness) from low category 2 (semi-attractive) down to high category 4 (somewhat unattractive). We were all bright and outgoing people with good senses of humor, polite manners, etc.. At the function, we initiated a conversation with Ms. X due to the fact that she was very attractive and lively (her attractiveness made her the target of our attention). We each spoke to her both as a group and then individually. I noted her overall reaction to each of us was one of mild to semi-interest, with the higher interest focused around Mr. Category 2 and the coolest reaction being registered upon Mr. Category 4. The mild reception was even noted by my friend who has the most exuberant and bubbly personality I've ever met, but was Mr. Average on the attractiveness scale. At this time our acquaintance Mr. Williams entered, displaying noteworthy high category 1 appearance, charm, and poise. In no time flat Ms. X lost all interest with our group and channeled more enthusiasm toward Mr. Williams than we had seen the entire night. Within no more than ten minutes they left together at (as I later found out) her request, for sexual company. Just a shallow person you might say? But Ms. X was engaged and carried a reputation of being very devoted and faithful to her fiancee prior to that lone encounter.

Mr. Williams and Ms. X eventually went on to marry each other. An isolated instance? Not hardly. I've witnessed (and you probably have to) this "selective warmness", whereby the reception and enthusiasm provided a person of the opposite sex is directly proportional to their appearance category. This example is another indication that people from all walks of life and backgrounds seek the most attractive mate possible.

While lower categories are not afforded the number of opportunities that more attractive persons are, factors such as pleasant nature or humorous personality, intelligence, interesting character, and individual accomplishments many times make up for a basic lack of total beauty. However, reliance on non-appearance factors is far more difficult simply because people often use a minimum acceptable level of appearance to determine whether to form a relationship.

Appearance Rule #6

"WOMEN & MEN alike use appearance or attractiveness as the INITIAL discriminator to determine whether to socialize, date, and even marry. Once a (perceived) minimum acceptable level of appearance has been met, other relevant factors such as sense of humor, kindness, honesty, wealth, power, etc. enter in."

The proofs for rule #6 are:

1) How many women have you known that have said the following regarding a very nice, responsible, intelligent, and financially secure man, "He is very nice, but I'm just not attracted to him?"

2) How many men have you known that have said the following regarding a very nice, well educated, responsible woman: "She's not my type", "She's too heavy", "She's just OK?"

3) How many men or women have you known that stated as the FIRST factor regarding a person of the opposite sex: "He's cute, hot, got a nice body, built, gorgeous" "She's sexy, got nice buns, nice breasts, hot, pretty?"

You're far less likely to hear the first thing mentioned about a potential relationship being "He/She has a nice personality, has a good job, is well educated, etc.." If you fail the attractiveness test, you'll likely not get a second chance with your non-appearance factors!

Even Charles Darwin in 1871 recognized that a mate is selected based upon appearance by stating:

> "In civilized life, man is largely, but by no means
> exclusively, influenced in the choice of his wife by
> external appearance."

In summary, persons of higher attractiveness are afforded a far greater opportunity to date, form loving relationships, and marry than less attractive persons. These persons have what it takes to get past the "attractiveness gate", if they so desire. Less attractive persons must work much harder or improve their appearance to make strides in forming relationships.

B. HOW YOUR APPEARANCE AFFECTS YOUR ABILITY TO SELECT A COMPATIBLE MATE

1) ATTRACTIVE—TOO MANY DATES

Suppose an attractive person dates a lot of persons and is used to several dates per week. Many would be envious of such luck. One burden these people carry though is that they have an almost unlimited supply of attractive persons pursuing them whereby there seems no need to "settle for second best." They develop an almost pompous attitude thinking they can have anyone they want most any time they want. They may either become bored with dating persons of the opposite sex or become cocky and callused and start to discourage a segment of the "pursuers." The psychology here is one of plentiful supply. Just imagine that you have access to free food all the time and never need to worry about that supply being cut off. You would, after time, become interested in gourmet foods, the nuances of aroma, flavor, texture, etc.. In short, you'd become more choosy about what you ate. The same principle applies to very attractive persons with a seemingly limitless supply of dates.

Next, comes the burden of comparison. Say, for example, that an attractive person has dated 100 persons thus far and continues to date. Perhaps date #34 was the best sexually of the first 100, but date #95 was the nicest and would do anything asked of them, and lastly, date #66 was the most intellectually stimulating. I'd hate to be date #101, #155, #267, etc. and be compared to all the preceding dates! This attractive person would have to feel they are "settling for a person less than totally desirable" if Mr. or Ms. Right was not the "best of the best." This poor person could search a long time unless they prioritize exactly what they are looking for in a potential mate

2) UNATTRACTIVE—TOO FEW DATES

Suppose you are unattractive and have had very few dates during your dating years. Here we have the opposite problem of the very attractive person in that unattractive persons may find it difficult to obtain even one date for the week and constantly wonder when their next date may be. They tend to linger in relationships where they know their partner incompatible, but stay together anyway so they won't be lonely until the next date. Persons in this situation have a "short supply mentality", whereby they tend to stay with incompatible partners longer than they should, and may agree to date and even marry incompatible persons for fear that they will end up alone, without companionship. Just imagine your food being in short supply. Would you worry about whether it was gourmet or had the right aroma? Not hardly! You'd accept just about anything edible and not be very selective at all. The same principle holds true for a person with the desire to date but finds a short supply of partners. These people will likely accept any available dates and are likely to "hang on" to these persons whether or not they are right for them. We have long called this "settling." These unattractive persons need to aggressively pursue dates based on the qualities they most value in a mate. Being complacent or withdrawing from the dating scene will most surely guarantee failure in finding a compatible mate.

3) BALANCING RELATIONSHIPS WITH SELECTIVITY AND INTUITION

a) Attractive persons

Attractive persons, due to their popularity and constant presence on the dating scene need to be selective. They should resist the temptation to date for the sake of dating, and avoid taking advantage of pursuers for money, favors, sex, and power. It would be easy for an attractive person to be lured into a situation whereby they get comfortable with the wealth, power, or influence of their mate. The attractive person should be very intuitive and careful that they are not being "roped" into a situation whereby their mate is merely infatuated by their appearance. They must ensure that their mate possesses the same qualities that they themselves value whereby they will be truly happy with this one person the rest of their life. In short, the attractive person must have the integrity to forego the lure of convenient or self-fulfilling relationships versus relationships which truly bring happiness, compatibility, and balance. Attractive people, as the saying goes, really do need "to beat them off with a stick!"

b) Unattractive Persons

Unattractive persons, due to their lack of appeal toward the opposite sex, also need to be selective in that they should not settle for just any relationship that comes along. They must be wary of the "short supply" syndrome and overcome the urge to settle down with whomever is available versus waiting for Mr. or Ms. Right. Unattractive persons should (and usually do) put their energy into increasing their exposure to relationships, accentuating their non-appearance related qualities (i.e. personality, education, power, wealth, sense of humor, etc.), and generally improve their AQ (Chapter 4). Unattractive persons need the integrity and inner strength to terminate incompatible relationships despite the disheartening prospect of loneliness. They must resist the temptation of staying in a relationship where they are comfortable simply because their mate is a good provider, is more attractive, or has lots of money. Unattractive persons need to recognize when a situation has formed based solely on availability or convenience. They must aggressively pursue relationships; working harder than persons of higher appearance categories, with more charm, poise, and tact than displayed the so-called more attractive persons. I've seen instances where the unattractive person, who aggressively displayed their charm and good personality, outmaneuvered the meek, shy, attractive person. It does happen!

c) Average Persons

Persons of average attractiveness, due to their large numbers in relation to all other categories, actually have the easiest time in selecting a mate. At 66% of the population, persons of average attractiveness (Category 3) have the greatest number of people with similar appearance to select from. A person of average appearance actually has an advantage over their more (or less) attractive counterparts. Average persons need not worry about limited supply as do their less attractive counterparts. They can, if they choose to, select a mate within their own category, have many dates, and find a person who is genuinely compatible. They can usually find a date and tend to avoid the "short-supply" mind-set of their less attractive counterparts. Average persons also need not worry about being pursued solely due to their external beauty as do their more attractive counterparts. Average persons are more assured of attracting a mate based on a balance of appearance and non-appearance qualities such as internal beauty, intellectual appeal, compatibility, and background. In essence, average persons have the easiest time in mate selection, with far less chance of falling into the psychological traps of their (un)attractive counterparts. Average persons must, however, resist the temptation to settle with a less attractive pursuer simply due to ease of attainment. This could be a pitfall for a non-assertive or shy person of average appearance. While they possess the necessary appearance characteristics to attract another average person for a mate, their "exposure" is limited by their introversion and lack of presence on the dating scene. The selection of one less attractive by an average person could spell disaster in that the appearance incompatibility can directly affect how successful the overall long term relationship will be. (appearance incompatibility is discussed in the next section).

Average persons should be content on being average and just be themselves, rather than striving to secure a very attractive person solely just to bolster their own self-image. Many average persons succumb to the pressures of advertising and are driven to secure more attractive mates who are actually incompatible to their own appearance. Average persons might, for instance, secure a very attractive person as their mate overlooking non-appearance factors such as intelligence (hence the term attractive airheads), motivation, kindness, even compatibility. Relationships based solely on external factors and having secured an "attractive trophy" are likely doomed to failure over the long term.

In short, average persons have the greatest opportunity to be happy and secure in a relationship, but they need to resist the temptation to secure a mate based solely on the ease to attract a less attractive mate or the lure of obtaining higher social status through a more attractive mate. Persons of average appearance must attract a mate based on a balance of appearance and non-appearance related factors. Life-long happiness is the reward for maintaining this balance, while an unhappy or failed relationship awaits those who violate this delicate mate selection balance.

C. APPEARANCE COMPATIBILITY—HOW IT AFFECTS HOW WELL YOU ARE TREATED BY YOUR MATE.

The way you are treated in relationships is directly related to your appearance. Your treatment relates directly to a concept called Appearance Compatibility. Incompatibility in appearance between two persons in a relationship can cause much pain and mistreatment. Appearance incompatibility is simply the pairing of two persons where the appearance of one partner provides greater satisfaction than the appearance of the other partner. Since successful relationships are built on the concept of total sharing, mutual support, and mutual benefit, the average net effect of all factors should provide equivalent levels of satisfaction. One factor of relationship satisfaction is your mate's appearance. If your appearance category is much higher than your mate's, other factors must offset the satisfaction deficit. This deficit will upset the relationship's equilibrium and jeopardize its longevity. The treatment by any partner in a relationship worsens as the satisfaction deficit increases. Research supports this equity/inequity theory.

Critelli and Waid in 1980 found that, "even though there was an overall significant positive correlation for within couple attractiveness, that when their partners were the more attractive member of the dyad they loved their partners more and indicated greater submission in their relationships."

Consider the following real life scenarios, which we've all seen at one point or another, to better illustrate the Appearance Incompatibility concept:

ATTRACTIVE MALE SEEKING AN UNATTRACTIVE FEMALE:

Here, the first question that should come to anyone's mind, particularly the female in this case, is "what would motivate a person to seek a lower appearance category?" The female must be providing some sort of other benefit to account for the obvious appearance imbalance. Maybe the male is older and more mature and finds that the female, while unattractive, provides exactly the personality, companionship and goal compatibility which he desires. The female may also provide other satisfaction in the form of a pleasant personality, power, wealth, superior sexual performance, short-term sexual satisfaction, good home maker, etc.. The female will likely feel fortunate to be with one so attractive and will probably attempt to hang on to the relationship by attempting to make up for the appearance deficit in any way possible including...

1) Sex early in the relationship
2) Uninhibited sex
3) Extra pleasures and niceties
4) Wealth, Power, Status, provided to the male (if possessed by the female).

The female needs to be very cautious in this instance so as to not be taken advantage of by the more attractive male. I've seen many instances where the attractive male took advantage of the lesser attractive female. I've also seen countless instances where attractive, particularly younger or insecure men, use their appearance for the sole purpose of obtaining sexual favors from the often eager though less attractive female. The most important satisfaction provided to a male (particularly younger men) is sexual pleasure. Females should take care to not be so overwhelmed with the attractive person's appearance that they agree to engage in sex too early into the relationship. Older females seem to have learned the dangers presented by the "marauding attractive male" through experience, but younger females often become victims. They should date for a longer period to better determine the TRUE intentions of their more attractive pursuer, in particular avoiding the "one night stand."

Appearance Rule #7

"MEN will engage in short-term relationships with persons of lower appearance for the sole purpose of obtaining sexual favors. WOMEN typically will not engage in this type of behavior due to their tendency to want to make love, not merely have physical sex."

The proofs for rule #7 are:

1) How many men are familiar with the term "coyote ugly?" The term is known and used across the country to refer to the scenario where a man wakes up after a night of heavy drinking followed by sexual intercourse and suddenly "discovers" how ugly their female partner for the night was. The story goes on that they have to chew off their own arm in order to not wake the ugly partner and make their morning escape. Hence the term, "she was coyote ugly."

2) How many happy, long-term successful relationships have you encountered where the female was very unattractive and the male was attractive? I bet you will think of few of these instances.

3) How many older women avoid very attractive men because they are typically "jerks", pompous, manipulative, and poor partners?

Women, on the other hand, tend not to engage in this short term, sexually-focused behavior. Once a minimum level of appearance acceptability has been established with a prospective male (remember rule #6), women tend to place more emphasis on factors such as honesty, personality, kindness, etc. than do men. Since men are typically the aggressors for sexual encounters, they tend to rely more heavily on appearance and how "turned on" they are by their female counterparts. Women, on the other hand, have strong maternal and family motivations and are more interested in how well a man will provide a stable family environment via his values, commitment, security, etc.. The most important factors to the female are that the man will be true to her, that he will be openly honest about his feelings, that he will be a good provider, and that he will be totally committed to his wife and family. The balance here is that if the female is compatible and sexually desirable she provides the male with sufficient pleasure to remain with the relationship. In return for this satisfaction level, the man will remain committed to the relationship and provide the non-appearance related satisfaction that the female seeks.

Appearance Rule #8

"WOMEN in general tend to place more emphasis on factors such as personality, status, sincerity, honesty, kindness, and openness than appearance than do men."

The proofs for rule #8 are:

1) How many women do you know say that the most important factor about a man is that he be HONEST, OPEN, SINCERE, etc..? Most women I know rate these non-appearance factors as very important.

2) How many women do you know, particularly older women who say "Appearance in a mate is not that important?" (the older a women is the less likely she is to focus on appearance) Once a minimum level of appearance satisfaction has been met with a man, the non-appearance factors are rated very important.

3) Do you notice that men typically talk more about sex, women's anatomy or appearance than do women about men's? Do you also notice that women typically have many more conversations about relationships, emotional issues, and commitment, than do men?

ATTRACTIVE FEMALE WITH AN UNATTRACTIVE MALE:

In the second instance of appearance incompatibility we have an attractive female seeking an unattractive male. Just as in the case of the attractive male seeking the unattractive female, the question that comes to mind, is what would motivate the female to seek a lower appearance category? The male must be providing some sort of other benefit to account for the imbalance in levels of appearance satisfaction. Maybe the female is older and more mature and finds that the male, while unattractive, provides exactly the personality, companionship and goal compatibility that she desires. Maybe the male is very financially secure, powerful, strong, or he reminds the female of her father. The more insecure the female, the more likely she will be seeking to obtain a financially secure male in order to provide a safe and secure home with the security she is lacking. Also a female who lacked a strong father figure during her upbringing, might seek to obtain a male who resembles or reminds her of her father. The female, in these cases where she is seeking to obtain a father figure or secure provider, will most likely worry much less about the male's appearance. In the case where women diminish the importance of appearance, in order to secure a financially secure or father figure male, appearance rule #9 applies.

Appearance Rule #9

Insecure, older WOMEN, who lacked a strong father figure during childhood, tend to select older, powerful, dominant men rather than very attractive men. These women feel safer, more secure and compensated for their own lack of identity through this powerful/dominant mate."

The proofs for rule #9 are:

1) How many attractive women do you know that are with unattractive men but men who are celebrities, wealthy, or powerful? Many examples come to my mind.

2) How many times have you seen women pursuing men that weren't very attractive due to their money, position, or celebrity status? What about followers of rock groups, TV/Motion Picture celebrities, sports stars or persons who married them?

3) Have you ever seen or heard of instances where a women has married a man because the man closely resembles or reminds her of her father?

4) Have you ever seen young, attractive women with much older men? Many times these men are financially secure, influential, powerful, or father figures. The commonly known term "SUGAR DADDY" refers to an older male taking care of a very attractive younger female.

D. HOW AGE AFFECTS YOUR ABILITY TO SELECT A COMPATIBLE MATE

It is said that with age comes experience. The same holds true regarding mate selection. In general, the younger you are the more you tend to rely on appearance as a determinant of whether or not to form a relationship and often confuse physical infatuation with true love. A young person will more readily equate attractive appearance to happiness, good life, compatibility, etc.. Due in large to their limited number of experiences, they haven't learned that both good and bad people come in all shapes, sizes, and appearances. They want to maximize the appearance of their mate; marry a "White Knight or "Super-Model." Some would say that "love is blind." Love of a person's appearance without regard to many other important qualities is most definitely blind. Appearance rule #10 applies to the "blind" person who relies heavily on appearance alone for mate selection.

Appearance Rule #10

The younger a person is the more he/she tends to rely on attractiveness as the key factor in determining whether to enter into a relationship."

Proofs for appearance rule #10 are:

1) How many times have you seen relationships fail between people who married at a young age? How many times have you asked "Why did you marry him?", and the answer was that "he was cute", "handsome", or "nice looking?" I've heard it countless times.

2) How many older, more secure men and women actually stray away from very attractive persons because of some past unpleasant experience they had? Can you say the same about younger persons?

3) How many times have you heard teenagers say "He's so cute", "She's foxy", or "He's a hunk?" Do you hear the same comments from older folks? Probably a lot less often.

4) How many younger men & women have you known that flat out refused to talk with you because you failed their appearance "test?" Older men and women are much more likely to give you an opportunity to talk a while and also give you a more polite "good-bye" if they're not interested.

E. HOW YOUR (IN)SECURITY AFFECTS YOUR ABILITY TO SELECT A COMPATIBLE MATE

As most people age, they tend to get wiser and realize that factors such as kindness, goals, values, ideology, ambition, and personality matter just as much, if not more, than one's appearance does in mate selection. This transition only occurs if the individual, while aging, becomes secure about who they are as a person. If they fail to feel secure about themselves, they will likely continue to rely heavily on appearance factors alone for mate selection. They tend to judge their accomplishments based on attractive "conquests" or how attractive their mate appears. People who rely totally on external appearance factors for satisfaction are very shallow. The removal of the external pleasure by aging, gaining weight, etc. removes all pleasure entirely. The relationship, like the shallow-rooted tree, simply blows away since it was not deeply rooted and based on factors deep within (i.e. beliefs, faith, etc.).

APPEARANCE IS EVERYTHING

Appearance Rule #11

"Insecure, older MEN & WOMEN continue to rely on attractiveness as the key factor in determining whether to form a relationship with the opposite sex."

Proofs for appearance rule #11 are:

1) Do you ever see older men riding around in sports cars with very young women riding alongside? Are these men secure? Hardly!—They have something to prove, rather than form a serious relationship.

2) Ever hear about older, divorced women who date or have "flings' with much younger men? Are these women secure? About as secure as a floating dock!

3) Ever hear about older men leaving their wives for younger, more attractive women? Maybe the marriages were incompatible, but many times they're in for another big disappointment by likely relying too heavily again on appearance.

4) What types of women go to male strip shows? Are these women secure in their relationships? Maybe some are, but I'm willing to bet that most are older, very infatuated with a man's appearance, and unsuccessful in finding a compatible mate themselves!

Insecure men, in addition to selecting a mate based exclusively on appearance, sometimes feel the need to secure a female mate who is non-assertive and unintelligent in order to stand out as the more dominant mate. These men, needing to feel dominant, select very attractive (but less intelligent) mates so they may be able to assert total authority in the relationship and appear dominant to their peers from having secured a very attractive female (trophy). These female mates can be easily manipulated since they, like their male counterparts, have very low self-esteem, allowing themselves to be manipulated. Both the female and the male have relied on appearance for mate selection and are committed to each other for the superficial satisfaction which provides equilibrium to the basic insecurity in their own personalities. Here, the attractive mate provides a sense of security and accomplishment in an otherwise unaccomplished life. Appearance rule #12 comes readily to mind in this instance.

Appearance Rule #12

"Insecure MEN seek more attractive, yet inferior in intellect and stature, women. In this manner, these men stand out as the dominate partner and appear, in a microcosm, to be a person of accomplishment (i.e. a good provider with an attractive mate)."

Proofs for appearance rule #12 are:

1) Have you ever heard of a man having a "mid-life crisis?" These men will typically

leave a long-term relationship for a younger, more attractive person. The women they often secure are often referred to as a "Dumb Dolly" (a very young and attractive, yet totally unintelligent and naive female). These men need to feel that they are still attractive and must feel intelligent in a relationship. What better way for them to stand out than to contrast themselves against a very attractive, unintelligent female partner?

2)   The Sugar Daddy mentioned in rule #9 also applies here. Some men need a younger and more attractive mate due to their own insecurity. The younger female in turn needs an older, more secure (emotionally & financially) man due to their insecurity. The match balances these needs based on insecurities. Needless to say, these relationships are generally short-lived.

3)   How many times have you met a very attractive man with a very attractive, yet totally uninteresting or unintelligent female? If you have, then my bet is the male is very insecure.

Older, more secure persons, on the other hand, realize that in order for their relationship to be successful, they must balance appearance, compatibility, and other non-appearance factors. You can't live a happy life with a category 1 (beautiful person), but who basically has nothing in common and treats you unfavorably. You can, however, get along with someone somewhat unattractive who treats you like gold, helps you in every way they can, and would literally "give you the shirt off their back" (especially if you are older, more mature, and more secure). You might even find a dreamy existence really does exist, and that your "White Knight", while physically unattractive, is beautiful inside. Remember the phrase, "beauty is only skin-deep?"

Appearance Rule #13

"Secure MEN & WOMEN tend to shift from appearance to factors such as lifetime goals, ability to interact, and intellectual compatibility in mate selection."

Proofs for appearance rule #13 are:

1)   How many times have you or a friend been "burned" by a very attractive partner who was pompous, arrogant, or just down right rude? Persons who have experienced this learn that having a very attractive mate also has many pitfalls and isn't as appealing or glamorous as it first seems!

2)   As you get older, don't you find yourself looking more toward family, what you have accomplished thus far in life, and how you have treated other people? What do these thoughts have to do with a person's appearance?—ABSOLUTELY NOTHING!

3) As you get older, do factors such as how a person treats you, or gets along with you overshadow their appearance? I certainly find this to be true.

F. APPEARANCE AND THE PERFECT MATE

You would probably agree that the perfect mate is someone you can trust totally, talk to very freely, confide in anytime, and generally feel good and comfortable around at all times. You feel comfortable with their appearance and they feel comfortable with yours. The perfect mate will probably be somebody who falls into the same appearance category and has very similar features to yourself. Let's face it, nobody's appearance is more comfortable to view than your own. If your mate has similar appearance features, won't you be most comfortable with those features similar to yours? That is precisely why you see so many couples with very similar features. Short people tend to partner with other short people, tall people tend to partner together, heavy people tend to partner with other heavy persons, thin persons hook up with other thin persons, etc.. In fact, some of the happiest relationships I've seen have been between persons who could have passed for brother and sister.

Just imagine some of the anxieties experienced by a heavy person matching with a thinner person and undressing for the first time to make love. The heavier person is likely to feel very uncomfortable and self-conscience about undressing in front of their thinner partner. The thinner person probably engages in some sort of physical activity, while the heavier person probably does not. The thinner person may be more health conscious, more active, etc.. The appearance differences alone point toward potential personality and life-style differences which would compound any incompatibility in appearance. In short, a generally uncomfortable relationship.

Also think of the ridicule a short man receives when he dates a very tall lady. He is likely to feel inferior and she may feel unprotected. How may times have you seen tall women with short guys in a long term relationship? I'm sure there are some, but they are rare situations. These people are also likely to be uncomfortable.

When was the last time you saw a model (category 1) with an very unattractive person? How many comments can you conjure up about what other people say about such a situation? Remember the 1970's hit song entitled, "IS SHE REALLY GOING OUT WITH HIM?" by Joe Jackson? This song was devoted entirely to pretty women going out with "gorillas" and less attractive men. The song made statements such as "Something is going wrong around here", "Is she really going to take him home tonight?", and many more comments which pointed to the obviously dissimilar appearance categories between the man and woman.

Other comments regarding an unattractive person being with an attractive person such come readily to mind:

1) "What does he/she see in him?"

2) "He/She is just probably going out with each other because he/she has money, power, etc.."

3) "I'm really surprised at him/her. She/he can do so much better than that (person)!"

4) "I feel bad for him/her. He/She is going out with such a beast."

Will either of these persons feel comfortable going out with the other? The unattractive person probably always wonders why he/she deserves someone so attractive and worries that another more attractive person will attempt to steal their mate away. The attractive person will have to succumb to many lures of relationships with persons of similar or higher appearance than their mate (especially and more frequently if the pursuers notice how unattractive the present mate is). They'll likely think to themselves "what am I doing with this unattractive person?", particularly if things go awry in the relationship. Again, this is a very uncomfortable situation whereby tensions, anxieties, and fears run high in the relationship.

The key to selecting the perfect mate is to be comfortable with your own appearance and select someone very similar in appearance. Appearance rule # 14 directly applies in this instance.

Appearance Rule #14

"Successful relationships (friends, marriage, dating) are generally formed between people of extremely close appearance (female height usually shorter than male height by about 10%, weight similar for given frame, similar hair color, etc.)."

Proofs for appearance rule #14 are:

1) How many couples can you point to where the one mate is totally different than the other in height, weight, frame, etc.. How many can you point to where they are similar? My research has placed the numbers at roughly an 11% to 89% split, respectively. Try sampling your friends and acquaintances. I think you'll find similar results.

2) How many unsuccessful relationships have you had? Ever wonder or speculate what factor appearance incompatibility played in the relationship not succeeding? My findings point to the fact that it probably played a definite role.

3) Who do you feel more comfortable with, a mate of similar or dissimilar appearance? I personally feel much more comfortable with someone of very close personal appearance to my own. As a matter of fact, I am married to someone with very similar body features, weight, hair color, facial features, etc.. Why? Because I'm most comfortable with a person of similar traits. You probably are also.

APPEARANCE IS EVERYTHING

Research tends to uphold the similar appearance theory as well:

> *"C. Hill, Rubin, and Peplau (1976) noted that*
> *steady dating couples who were dissimilar in physical*
> *attractiveness have broken up 2 years later, whereas*
> *those couples of similar attractiveness had tended to*
> *remain together."*

"White in 1980 also found that within-dating-couple similarity in physical attractiveness was predictive of courtship progress. He found serious' daters and those who were engaged or married to more similar to their partners in independently rated attractiveness than were casual daters. White also found 9 months later that those casually or seriously dating couples who had stayed together." (p. 28 The Social Psychology of Facial Appearance.)

It is critical that you first know your appearance category, accept your category and overall appearance in order that you don't chase after people who you aspire to become (thinner, taller, bigger, etc.), and then feel less than totally comfortable after you finally form a relationship with these persons. If you don't recognize and accept your appearance or change it (your appearance) to that which you accept first, you fail to create a comfortable situation for yourself. Therefore, how can you be comfortable with anyone else? Like the old saying, "If you can't love yourself, you're not likely to love anybody else." The same applies to your appearance. Be comfortable and feel good about your appearance, then select somebody who makes you feel totally comfortable in terms of the way you look at them and the way they look at you. A mate of very similar appearance contributes immensely toward forming a lasting, compatible, and most importantly, a comfortable and anxiety-free relationship.

Official Findings Support the "Similar Appearance Mate" Rule:

Reader's Digest: Sexual Chemistry—11/93
"Scientists have long known that people typically choose mates who closely resemble themselves in build and intelligence."

Boston Globe: America's Sexual Myths—10/13/94
"Americans meet, date and mate people from their own socioeconomic circle. If they see someone across a crowded room, it's likely to be a room crowded with friends and colleagues and people like them."

Journal of Social Psychology R. Bailey & Price Researchers—1978
"Individuals entered into dating and maintained a dating relationship only with partners whom they perceived as supporting their own self-concept of physical attractiveness."

G. APPEARANCE, LONG-TERM RELATIONSHIPS, AND MARRIAGE

After you have selected the perfect mate and settled down with an appearance-compatible partner, a very interesting phenomenon occurs. As you live your lives together, you learn from each other and share more and more of life's experiences. Over time, each mate starts picking up the other's habits, temperament, thoughts, language, and ideas. Just like when you lived with your parents, you start absorbing the qualities of the one that influences your life the most—your mate. You begin to literally become a single entity—totally merged in actions, mind, and spirit. I've also noticed that couples who have been together for a long time tend to appear like one another. As we found in D, "APPEARANCE AND THE PERFECT MATE", successful relationships are usually formed between persons of very similar appearance. Many people have indicated to me that couples tend to appear more like one another over time. The question then is whether the couple looked like each other to begin with and age in a like manner, or whether some natural selection phenomenon occurs whereby people married a long period of time start appearing like one another. It's possible that the total absorption of ideas, temperament, mannerisms, etc. between mates actually has an outward affect on appearances. There are examples in nature where birds, animals, and fish assume the appearance of their mate. Can it be possible that humans are subject to this same phenomenon? It would make a very interesting Darwin-like study of natural selection and adaptation. Whatever the underlying reason, appearance rule #15 applies directly to this situation.

Appearance Rule #15

"Couples tend to talk, act, and more incredibly APPEAR more alike over time."

Proofs for appearance rule #15 are:

1) Have you been in a long term relationship with somebody and started to talk like your mate? Ever remember saying "Oh my word—I'm even starting to sound like you" to someone you've been involved with for a long period of time? If so, your speech actually started to merge with your mate's.

2) Have you ever rectified something that previously irked your mate? Started being more clean/tidy, became more open about voicing your feelings, became less frugal/less extravagant? Your mate was probably asking you to change your ways because it bothered him/her. Why? Most likely because they(your mate) were clean, open, generous, etc.. If you indeed fixed or changed this situation, you merged toward your mate's actions and started to act more like your mate.

3) How many persons do you know who have been married for a long time and appear dissimilar? They probably look and act very similar to each other.

4) How different is your appearance to your mate's? Ask others how similar (or different) you appear. Ask them if you look more alike now than when you first met. I bet you look very similar if you've been together for a long time.

H. APPEARANCE AND YOUR ABILITY TO MAKE FRIENDS

Have you ever noticed that persons of similar appearance tend to socialize together? Very attractive model types tend to socialize with other very attractive persons. Unattractive persons tend to socialize exclusively with other unattractive persons (if they socialize at all). Average persons are a little more versatile in that they tend to socialize mostly with average persons, yet have been known to travel at times with low category 2's or high category 4's. Of course, other factors affect the reasons why people decide to socialize with certain groups of people such as wealth, status, intelligence, background, etc.. One of the more critical of the factors that fuels the decision to socialize or not is a person's appearance. Why might this be, you ask? The reason is mostly hidden by our subconscious, simply mental comfort. Take for instance, that a very attractive category 1 model went out with a category 5 for a day. The category 1 would be deluged, as usual, with smiling faces, people wanting to say hello, friendly greetings from storekeepers, acquaintances, etc.. In the same instance, the category 5 is met with the usual cool reception or is totally ignored by the same people who are warming to the category 1. Here, the category 1 probably feels very uncomfortable in that they are receiving this attention and their less attractive acquaintance is not.

Being with the category 5 illuminates the disparity in treatment that they are receiving relative to other (less attractive persons.) This naturally makes the category 1 feel very uncomfortable. The category 5, on the other hand, probably feel angry or very awkward since such a disparity exists between the treatment provided to the category 1 and themselves. This illumination makes the encounter for the day painful and uncomfortable. The category 5 would probably like to withdraw from the social scene for a time and is not likely to socialize with a category 1 or 2 again, at least in the immediate future! They would probably feel much more comfortable socializing with another category 4-5, who receives the same societal treatment as themselves and who provides a safe haven for denying that any appearance and societal treatment gap exists. By not being around the category 1, there is no treatment difference. The treatment difference simply (in their minds) disappears.

The category 1 would probably feel much more comfortable being around more happy, outgoing persons than the category 5. The category 1-2's often assume that, since the category 4-5's are so reserved, they would rather be around more outgoing persons. These outgoing persons are likely to be other category 1-2's, since society, by their favorable treatment of the attractive persons, encourages their positive attitude. You too, would probably be friendly and outgoing if persons you encountered were friendly, encouraging, went out of their way to make your acquaintance, and smiled at you upon making eye contact.

Category 5's, on the other hand, are encouraged to withdraw from society since few people want to make their acquaintance, often avoid encounters with them, and provide a cool reception when they absolutely have to have an encounter with them. You would probably be reserved, withdrawn, and maybe even angry if such treatment was provided to you! No wonder the category 1's are usually outgoing, friendly, and popular. They are constantly encouraged and provided positive treatment. Likewise, it is no small wonder that category 5's withdraw, avoid encounters with others, and are generally unhappy. Society reinforces and encourages the category 5 to be introverted, shy, withdrawn, and possibly angry by its generally negative treatment.

In short, people tend to stay with those whom they feel comfortable around. People will probably socialize with persons of very similar appearance who will likely receive the similar societal appearance treatment. Unattractive persons stay hidden or with others who receive the same negative treatment in order to forget (deny) that more attractive persons are treated so much more favorably. Unattractive persons feel comfortable with other unattractive persons. Attractive persons, on the other hand, tend to socialize with other very attractive persons. They enjoy and are comfortable with those who are treated as favorably by society as they are. They feel uncomfortable with persons who are treated poorly by others and tend to attribute this poor treatment of the unattractive to personality related disorders. The assumption is that the personality disorder was a pre-existing condition. They fail to realize that appearance has a direct, if causal, affect on the unattractive person being more introverted.

Appearance Rule #16

"Persons of SIMILAR ATTRACTIVENESS tend to socialize with persons of similar attractiveness. Very attractive (category 1), moderately attractive (category 2), average (category 3), and below average (category 4/5) persons generally socialize with persons within their respective attractiveness categories."

Proofs for appearance rule #16 are:

1) How many extremely attractive model types (category 1's) do you know that socialize with very unattractive persons on a regular basis? Date, marry, have similar jobs, etc.?

2) How many instances at work, at the mall, or at a party, can you recall where persons of similar appearance were together? If you don't remember, take notice next time you're out. You may be astonished how many instances persons of similar appearance tend to congregate and socialize together.

3) Think about your friends and those you socialize with on a regular basis. Are they generally similar in appearance? Chances are that they are similar to your own appearance category and that you feel comfortable when with them.

REAL LIFE EXAMPLE OF RULE #16:

A friend of mine was born into a family of four children. He happened to be the most attractive one of the four, being a high category 2. The other children of the family ranged in appearance from low category 3 to low category 4. As the children of this family grew up, tensions mounted between the category 2 and the others because he (the category 2) was afforded better treatment from the parents, neighbors, and school acquaintances. Also, the disparity between the number of dates my friend received compared to the other children was very obvious. The other three children would often vent their frustration toward their brother with comments such as the following:

* The brothers would ask, "How come you get all the nice looking girls?"
* "What did you do to deserve a part in the school play?"
* "You can't play with us, your hair might get messed up."
* "He gets away with murder around here" (to the parents).

As the tension and frustration mounted between the children, there was a slow and gradual isolation and withdrawal by the category 2 to seek his own friends, and minimize the interaction with the other three children. Mr. Category 2 made friends with other attractive persons, dated very attractive girls, and was afforded many opportunities at school and in after school jobs. The division between the children grew after Mr. category 2 was offered a good paying sales job while in his senior year of high school and went on to marry an extremely attractive woman. In talking with my friend he stated very clearly that the rest of the children were jealous of him and incorrectly thought that he was in a different league from his brothers & sister. He said that he honestly felt that he indeed was provided more opportunities and better treatment from others and his parents than were the other children. He also said that this "was not his fault, just merely the way it worked out."

One brother admitted to me one time, that he was very jealous of his brother and wished he could have had the same opportunities provided to him. He said he still loved his brother, but felt their lives were different enough to warrant limited interaction. In actuality, the three remaining siblings remained close to one another while the more attractive brother stayed within his own circle of friends who were, by no coincidence, all very attractive!

Mr. Category 2 also lost contact with people like myself as he got older, despite many attempts on my part to call, write, and stay in contact. I now have a better relationship with the other siblings, who are all within my appearance category.

While this might appear to be an extreme example where a family splits over appearance differences, there are many more common scenarios of appearance segregation. Take for instance, the case where heavy people lose a lot of weight and change their social circles radically toward a higher category. After losing weight, they are more accepted in other (higher) social circles, allowed to date persons previously uninterested, and are accepted by others more easily than when they were the same, but heavier, person.

Likewise, people who gain a lot of weight tend to lose contact with their old circle of more attractive friends. They find themselves socializing with less attractive persons who they feel more comfortable being around. This is not to say that all their friends will abandon them, but there are many shallow people who place a greater emphasis on a person's appearance than inner qualities. Countless stories tell of sociologists adorning inflating apparatus in order to appear anywhere from 50-100 pounds heavier. These sociologists are astounded how radically their treatment by society changes. These people haven't changed one iota of personality, education, intelligence, or level of societal contributions, yet they are now treated poorly and differently simply by appearing heavier. Draw your own conclusion.

CHAPTER 2 SUMMARY

A. Attractive persons have many more opportunities to date and form relationships than do unattractive persons of similar accomplishment and motivation.

B. People tend to maximize the attractiveness of their mate.

C. The first factor people use in determining whether to acquaint, date, or marry is a person's appearance.

D. Attractive persons need to resist the temptation to date many partners in order to avoid becoming over selective.

E. Unattractive persons need to resist the temptation to settle with an incompatible person simply from the fear of being alone or having to endure a tough dating scene.

F. Average persons have the greatest opportunity to select an appearance-compatible mate.

G. Selection of an appearance-compatible mate enhances your probability of being treated well by your mate.

H. Selection of an appearance-incompatible mate increases the chance that you will be treated poorly by your mate.

I. Younger persons tend to discriminate and select a mate based primarily on appearance more than older persons.

J. Insecure persons tend to discriminate and select a mate based primarily on appearance more than secure persons.

K. The perfect mate is most likely a person with very similar appearance to your own.

L. The longer couples are together the more they tend to act, talk, and APPEAR alike.

M. People tend to socialize and make friends with people of similar appearance and tend to exclude those of dissimilar appearance.

CHAPTER
3

CAREERS AND APPEARANCE

According to a study published in the Fall of 1993 by researchers at the University of Texas and Michigan State, attractive persons earn 12% more over a working career than do unattractive persons. Countless *professional* studies, have proven that attractive persons are consistently hired over unattractive persons of extremely similar capabilities. Appearance discrimination is highly pervasive in the workplace today, increasing in frequency, and occurs with little or no intervention by management, government, or private equality organizations. Your appearance has, or will, affect your chances for being hired, promoted, or getting a raise. Appearance discrimination thrives due to its difficulty to prove, its subjective nature, and the extreme difficulty associated with prosecuting (suing) an offender. This chapter was written to raise your awareness of this pervasive, unchecked form of workplace discrimination. It should be considered "required reading" for anyone wanting to get ahead in corporate America and be able to recognize and combat Appearance Discrimination in the workplace. You are the only person who can protect yourself. No government agency, private institution, or other person will stand against Appearance Discrimination aimed at you.

WHICH BUSINESSES ARE LIKELY TO DISCRIMINATE BASED ON YOUR APPEARANCE?

Your likeliness to be hired, fired (laid-off), promoted, or provided a raise is directly related to the type of business you work for and your appearance within this organization. This Appearance—Business Success relationship is stated in Appearance Rule #17.

Appearance Rule #17

"The more an organization or position deals with the public, the greater likelihood that an attractive person will be hired, promoted, and receive greater compensation than the less attractive person."

Proofs for appearance rule #17 are:

1. Would you hire an unattractive or an attractive person (of similar capabilities) to provide sales demonstrations, attend trade seminars and shows in attempting to

sell a product crucial to your company's success? Nineteen out of twenty people questioned said they would hire the attractive person. You probably would too!

2. Would appearance be a key factor for someone who you hired to landscape your yard? You most likely would rely on non-appearance factors such as reputation, references, and cost.

3. How many unattractive TV news anchors, actors, and actresses (including product commercials) have you seen? What would your reaction be to seeing an extremely unattractive person on a TV commercial trying to sell a product such as breakfast cereal, makeup, an automobile, vacation, etc.? You'd probably have some sort of negative reaction, unless the ad revolved around humor.

Appearance rule #17 states the obvious in that the more a business, or particular position within a business, deals with the public, the greater the chance that an attractive person will be retained for that position over an unattractive person. On the opposite side of the equation, companies and positions that deal very little with the public tend to discriminate less or not at all based on appearance. Organizations that deal with the public are very sensitive to placing their (organization's) "best face" forward. They literally demand people who are attractive, neat, lean, thorough, and intelligent to provide a positive (good) impression of the organization. If that person is sloppy, overweight, disorganized, and appears less intelligent, the customer may think the rest of the organization is much the same (poor quality, unresponsive, poorly managed, etc.). Just think of some terms which come to mind when describing an efficient, effective organization:

1) LEAN
2) PROFESSIONAL
3) RESPONSIVE
4) ORGANIZED
5) SHARP
6) ADAPTIVE
7) QUICK
8) RELIABLE

These terms also describe a person who presents themselves well in terms of their appearance, one who is cleanly dressed and attractive. Would you mention any of the above adjectives in reference to an overweight and unattractive person?

Based on appearance rule #17, the more a position deals with the public, the greater the chance that appearance discrimination will be present. The list is based on interviews of people where we asked the following question: "What occupations do you feel have the highest percentage of very attractive people?"

Before you look at the list, get a piece of paper and write down YOUR top ten occupations for attractive people. Do this exercise alone or better yet with your spouse, significant other, or group of friends. See how many occupations you selected that match the list our group came up with. I bet they'll be very close.

A. TOP TEN OCCUPATIONS WHICH EXPERIENCE APPEARANCE DISCRIMINATION

1. Model, Actor, Actress
2. Television Anchor, Weather Person, etc.
3. Public/Customer Relations Representative
4. Sales a) Marketing Representative b) Stock Broker/Financial Planner c) Real Estate/Insurance Broker d) Automobiles, Boats e) Retail—Boutiques f) College Admissions Representative
5. Host/Hostess, Waiter/Waitress, Bartender, Flight Attendant
6. Chief Executive Officer (CEO)/Executive Level Mgrs.
7. Hair Stylist, Cosmetologist.
8. Health & Fitness Trainer/Aerobics Instructor.
9. Receptionist
10. Politician

The underlying theme to all these positions, in addition to dealing with the public, is that they all require the person to influence others to buy, watch, assist, return for another visit, etc.. If you are in one of these occupations, you are very likely to be discriminated against (at some point) based on your appearance. Unattractive persons in these positions tend to find their career rapidly stagnated and tend not to receive promotions, pay raises, etc. as fast as do their attractive, yet equally competent, counterparts. The glass ceiling tends to be very low for unattractive persons in these type of positions and they are impeded from getting ahead (promoted) over more attractive persons. For example, it is highly likely that an engineer will be hired based primarily on competency factors other than his/her appearance. This same engineer will, however, reach that glass ceiling for promotion within a large organization when they must, for example, deal with customers, interface with the media, meet with the board of directors, etc. Similarly, unattractive people are often blocked from even being hired into these types of positions based solely on their appearance and regardless of their other qualifications. Most noteworthy appearance-related lawsuits have been filed in one of the above "top ten" occupations.

The same people were later asked to list occupations where appearance is not important and appearance discrimination is seldom practiced. The following list of occupations was developed:

B. TOP TEN OCCUPATIONS WHERE APPEARANCE DISCRIMINATION IS NOT TYPICALLY EXPERIENCED

1. Janitor/Custodian
2. Construction Worker
3. Farmer

4. Mechanic
5. Factory/Production Worker
6. Outdoor Laborer
7. Federal, State, Local Government Employee
8. Technician, Engineer, Lab Assistant
9. Research & Development
10. Miner

These occupations require very little interaction with the public and a person's appearance has minimal impact on the success of the job at hand. These occupations are labor-intensive as opposed to influence-intensive. It is more likely that an unattractive person will receive promotions based on ability rather than their appearance. Unattractive persons are said to have greater promotional "penetration" in these types of positions than do unattractive persons found in one of the ten most attractive occupations. For example, an unattractive construction worker is much more likely to be promoted to supervisor, foreman, and to other higher positions if they are competent than will an unattractive, yet talented, sales person. The relationship between the probability of entrance into, or advancement within, an occupation and the type of occupation is shown in chart 3.

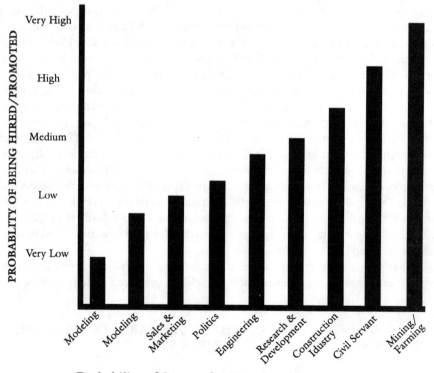

**Probability of Success for Unattractive Persons of
Similar Capabilities Per Industry**

Chart 3

Here we illustrate the relative chance for an unattractive person to gain employment or obtain a promotion within a given occupation provided an equal competence level. Chart 3 illustrates that the more a position relies on appearance factors for success, the greater the likelihood that appearance discrimination will occur. For example, modeling is highly reliant on appearance for a person to become successful (super model). Therefore, it is highly unlikely that an unattractive person would be hired, promoted, and be successful in a modeling career. Engineering, and Research & Development professions, which fall in the middle of the appearance discrimination spectrum, tend to value intelligence over appearance for their related positions. If you're in one of these occupations, you tend to be fairly insulated from appearance discrimination until you reach that glass, appearance-related "ceiling" involving positions which require much interaction with clients, top management, the media, etc.. Attractive Engineers or Scientists of equal competence, experience, and internal political affiliation will most likely be selected to interact with customers over their lesser attractive peers. Careers which are almost totally insulated from appearance discrimination are those where appearance is irrelevant to job success. Occupations such as mining and construction, which generally require physical strength and involve tasks which detract from physical appearance (workers get very dirty in performing these jobs), typically experience little (if any) appearance discrimination in regard to hiring and promotion.

C. THE PROMOTIONAL GLASS APPEARANCE CEILING

Many occupations in chart 3 are insensitive to a person's appearance regarding hiring. There does exist, however, a glass ceiling at which most unattractive persons will be blocked from promotion compared to their more attractive, yet equally competent, peers. While difficult to definitively prove, many organizations have been suspected of promoting only attractive people beyond a certain level within their organizations. While getting to middle management may be fairly easy, say within a large engineering organization, rising to senior/executive level management may require physical attractiveness as well as job competence, interpersonal skills, etc. We asked people to rate over 70 Fortune 500 CEO's on physical attractiveness from their photographs and rank them against the 1-5 scale we developed in chapter 1, based on quick, subjective ranking, vs. exact scoring for each executive. The results were astonishing and surprised even us. The following summarizes the results of this surprising study:

Appearance Quotient (AQ)	*# of CEOs*	*Percent*
Category 1 (Beautiful)	10	13%
Category 2 (Very Attractive)	55	74%
Category 3 (Average)	09	12%
Category 4 (Somewhat Unattractive)	01	01%
Category 5 (Very Unattractive)	00	00%

The results of our study show that 99% of all CEO's are average or above in attractiveness as rated by our survey respondents, and that over 87% are categorized as having a Very Attractive (Category 2) or Beautiful (Category 1) Appearance Quotient rating. This distribution falls in stark contrast to the standard Bell curve distribution for attractiveness throughout society. These numbers are, of course, skewed somewhat since the photographs were probably the "best of the best" pictures available, but are still rather remarkable nevertheless. The findings seem to indicate that many top managers (CEO's included) are selected from the ranks of attractive persons, or that being attractive is an unwritten prerequisite for putting the company's "best face forward." Most companies would deny the presence of appearance discrimination. What do you think? Remember, a large part of a CEO's job involves dealing with customers, the public, and the media. It stands to reason that the company will be sensitive to whom it places in such a high visibility position!

The survey results are particularly significant if your AQ puts you in something less than the Very Attractive category. In fact, they indicate that you have approximately a 13% chance of making it to CEO status versus a 87% chance for a Very Attractive or Beautiful person! Of course, many CEO's got to their position by being business smart, hard working, politically connected, intelligent, good public speakers, AND attractive. They had "ALL THEIR TICKETS PUNCHED" so to speak, and being attractive was simply one of those tickets. However, it should be clear that someone having all other "tickets punched" (i.e. hard working, intelligent, business smart, etc.), but who falls in AQ Category 4 or 5, has substantially less chance to reach the top (CEO) ranks of industry than does one with those same qualities PLUS an AQ of 1 or 2!

We asked a number of people if they thought this sort of distribution applied to their workplace for upper management persons. The response was overwhelmingly "YES!" Ask yourself the following questions to determine whether you are the victim of the glass appearance ceiling at your workplace:

1. Examine upper management and employees who frequently deal with the public or customer personnel. Rate alone, or preferably with a small group, each person in terms of the AQ ranking system in Chapter 1. What type of distribution do you find? If you find a high percentage of Very Attractive (Category 2) or Beautiful (Category 1) persons, a strong chance exists that appearance discrimination is present.

2. Take notice the next time a person is applying for promotion within your organization. Are persons selected for promotion consistently (or regularly) more attractive than their equally qualified peers? If you answer yes, appearance discrimination is likely to exist within your company.

3. Examine those selected for layoffs or "downsizing" demotions. Perform the same sort of appearance ranking performed in #1 above. What type of distribution do you arrive at? If you find a high percentage of persons who are below average (below Category 3), there is a strong chance that appearance discrimination exists at your workplace.

4. Examine the hiring practices at your current or prospective organization. Determine the type of organization you belong to or plan to join per the guidelines found in Section A and B of this chapter. Is your organization (occupation) likely

(similar to the Top 10) or unlikely (similar to the Bottom 10) to commit appearance discrimination? Examine the appearance distribution of persons working for this organization. What type of AQ distribution do you find? If you find a high percentage of persons above average (Category 2 or Category 1), there is a strong chance that appearance is important to this organization.

If you found, via questions 1-4 above, that your current or prospective organization is likely to, or is now, committing appearance discrimination, you should plan your course of action appropriately. You may want to "go with the flow" and actually improve your appearance (Chapter 7), or choose to fight this practice via the methods found later in this chapter.

D. WHY ATTRACTIVE PERSONS ARE FAVORED OVER UNATTRACTIVE PERSONS IN BUSINESS

Several documented studies show why attractive persons are treated more favorably by business organizations than their less attractive, yet equally qualified counterparts. The following are the principle reasons why attractive persons are treated more favorably by the business world. Each workplace appearance rule is followed by examples, research, quotes, and real-life examples of workplace appearance discrimination.

Appearance Rule #18
(workplace)

"Attractive persons have been found MORE EFFECTIVE in the art of persuasion (i.e. sales, marketing, public relations, TV commercials, etc.)."

Studies found that attractive persons generally influence others to listen, agree to and buy than do their less attractive peers. Studies such as the following provide proof of the greater influence that attractive persons (are believed to) possess:

1. In 1969, Sigall and Aronson wrote in the Journal of Experimental Social Psychology: "It is more rewarding to please a physically attractive person than one who is not attractive."

2. A 1971 study conducted by Snyder and Rothbart published in the Canadian Journal of Behavioral Science found that subjects who had listened to attractive presenters sided with the presenters' position much more favorably than when unattractive persons provided the same presentation.

3. In 1979, S. Chaiken found via a field study that Communicator attractiveness was found significantly to increase subjects' agreement with the communicators' position. It also had an almost significant effect on the number of subjects who agreed at the end of the interaction to sign a petition in line with the communicators' argument" (i.e. make the sale, close the deal, influence toward organization's goals).

APPEARANCE IS EVERYTHING

Proof for workplace Appearance Rule #18:

Ask yourself the following:

1) Think of persons who have influenced your decision-making process—buying your home, your car, or other major purchases. Think of someone whom you respect that is very influential. Is this person attractive and "put together" or are they less attractive and unkempt?

Appearance Rule #19
(workplace)

"Facially attractive people are EXPECTED to posses socially and organizationally desirable personality traits (i.e. warm nature, sensitive, etc.)."

Here, research points to the fact that attractive persons are expected to be more capable, honest, and generally more desirable than unattractive persons.

1) In 1972 Dion, Berscheid, and Walster "Found that FACIALLY attractive people were expected to be more likely to possess almost every socially desirable personality trait (e.g., warm, sensitive, kind, interesting, strong, sociable,)."

2) In 1979 Kupke, Hobbs, and Cheney "Found that females' evaluation of males they met for the first time were significantly affected by their (males) physical appearance."

Proofs for workplace Appearance Rule #19:

Ask yourself the following :

1) How attentive would you be to a presentation being given by a grotesque person? Think of your comfort level in this person's presence. On the opposite side of the coin, how attentive would you likely be to a presentation given by an equally competent person, but one who was strikingly attractive? If you are like the people we asked, you'd prefer the presentation given by the attractive person.

Appearance Rule #20
(workplace)

"Attractive persons are ASSUMED to possess greater ability in a particular job than unattractive persons."

Careers and Appearance

Research points to the fact that attractive persons are expected to be more capable, in performing work-related tasks, than unattractive persons. Studies such as the following provide incredible evidence of workplace preference toward the attractive over the unattractive person:

1) In 1977, researchers Tom Cash, B. Gillen, and S. Burns found that unattractive employees were viewed as more blameworthy than attractive persons for things that went wrong at the workplace. Since attractive persons were perceived as highly capable for a job, any explanation of their failure in these jobs was attributed to "lack of effort sufficient to demonstrate their inherent abilities."

2) The same researchers also found that "Both male and female assumed social desirability scores were lower for the unattractive than the moderately or higher attractive" when viewed from photographs. They also hypothesized, based on these findings, that "For neuter jobs, attractive applicants are more favorable than unattractive" and "attractive applicants are attributed greater overall employment potential than unattractive persons."

Proofs for workplace Appearance Rule #20:

Ask yourself the following:

1) Have you ever noticed that the high-paying, high-visibility jobs seem to be disproportionately staffed by attractive persons? Is this true at your workplace?

2) Which people in your organization have advanced quickly, so quickly in fact that their careers literally skyrocketed? Are these persons generally attractive or unattractive? (While not true in every instance, it is more generally true from our findings)

3) Refer back to our findings on the 70 CEO's in section D. A full 75% of them were above average (Beautiful, 2% and Very Attractive, 73%)!

The studies mentioned here are just a few of the hundreds of studies, research projects, and informal observations conducted which present evidence that ATTRACTIVE PERSONS HAVE A GREATER POTENTIAL FOR INFLUENCING OTHERS MORE EFFECTIVELY IN THE JOB MARKET AND WORKPLACE THAN DO UNATTRACTIVE PERSONS. In a business world that (more and more) deals with selling, negotiating and mediating, an attractive person will likely be viewed as more desirable for countless influence-related positions.

E. HOW TO RECOGNIZE, COMBAT, AND OVERCOME WORKPLACE APPEARANCE DISCRIMINATION

Now that we have established the fact that workplace appearance discrimination exists (more so in certain occupations), let's examine ways of combating and overcoming this potentially career-limiting issue. We'll examine how to recognize appearance discrimination, what action(s) to take, and where to get help.

1. RECOGNIZING WORKPLACE APPEARANCE DISCRIMINATION:

There are some basic steps to take in recognizing whether or not appearance discrimination is occurring at your workplace. We'll take you through a step-by-step approach for recognizing this (seldom discussed) form of workplace discrimination.

a) Appearance "climate" set by management (your boss)

Examine the actions, style, and appearance atmosphere created by your organization's leader or leaders. Your organization's top managers determine your business "climate and culture." They establish hiring practices, promotion policy, and work assignments. To understand the appearance climate at your present or potential workplace, you must first understand it's propensity for and sensitivity toward appearance, which will be largely dependent on the type of business as determined in section B. Beyond that is your manager's maturity and how conscious he/she is of their own appearance within the workplace. The following (workplace) appearance rules (21-22) apply to your boss(es).

Appearance Rule #21
(workplace)

"The less mature, more autonomous, or less educated a manager is within a given organization, the MORE LIKELY the chance that they will hire/fire/promote/assign responsibility based on factors other than inherent ability (i.e. appearance, friendship, sex, race, religion, etc.)."

Proofs for workplace Appearance Rule #21:

Ask yourself the following:

1) What would your comments be about a male boss who hires marginally competent, big-busted blondes? Would you think him to be a mature person looking out for the good of the company? I think not.

People we asked had the following comments about this hypothetical boss:
a) "Immature"
b) "Self-Centered"
c) "Egotistical"
d) "Jerk"
e) "Hasn't Grown Up"

2) Would you think that managers who have to report upward to multiple managers, or who are controlled by a hiring or promotion board, would practice appearance or sex discrimination? How about an autonomous boss with very little upward accountability (i.e. already a business owner, top level manager, etc.) would be more likely to be tempted to "do as they pleased" in the workplace? We found most sexual discrimination suits related to situations where bosses thought they had either free reign, with little or no involvement by other managers in the hiring process.

Appearance Rule #22
(workplace)

"The more a manager is consumed by their own appearance, the MORE LIKELY they will concern themselves with, and discriminate against, YOURS."

Proofs for workplace Appearance Rule #22:

Ask yourself the following (really stop and think about situations in your present or former workplace which apply):

1) Have you ever had bosses that dressed very sharply and who were always grooming and "making sure they looked just right?" Were these bosses ignorant of others' appearance in the workplace? We were amazed how many people told us that the bosses who were very concerned about their own appearance were those most likely to set dress standards, make comments about others' appearance, and most likely to commit appearance discrimination!

Your organization's management sets the acceptable levels of any behavior, including appearance discrimination. The more a manager is concerned with or consumed by appearance, the more likely appearance discrimination will be tolerated, even practiced regularly. Other than observance of your managers appearance, how do you determine if appearance discrimination really exists and is not just a "figment of your imagination?" The answer lies in data collected from different sources. Similar "intelligence gathering" activity can be used to combat many forms of discrimination (sex, race, age, etc.).

1) Intelligence Gathering on Appearance Discrimination

a) WRITTEN RECORDS/EXPLICIT STATEMENTS
Written and verbal appearance-related statements are, while most important in recognizing the existence of appearance discrimination, the most difficult evidence to obtain. Managers seldom write down anything which might be self-incriminating. Intelligence gathering on your manager's discriminatory behavior can be typically accomplished by obtaining various pieces correspondence provided to co-workers which might reveal a management appearance standard or actual discriminatory words, thoughts, statements. If you can obtain such written documentation regardomg a par-

ticular manager's thoughts on appearance, consider yourself very lucky (or the manager not very bright). The most effective way to construct a viewpoint on the manager's thoughts of the importance of appearance is via his/her direct comments made to yourself or others. By carefully piecing together these statements made to you and other friends at work, you can get a clear picture of the overall workplace appearance climate. Many managers tend to let down their guard in informal settings without the inhibitions of the work environment. Many people have found the true essence of their boss at holiday parties or other off-site encounters. The following is a true life example of one such encounter:

Stacey's boss, Mike, attended a holiday party. He was cordial to everyone present and "made the rounds" to greet and speak with everyone. Several hours passed, Mike's senior managers left, and drinks continued to flow freely. Stacey, who is extremely attractive, decided to join in the conversation with Mike and others. After several minutes, Mike and Stacey found themselves alone talking about workplace and holiday issues. At that point, the conversation turned to Stacey's performance with a particular customer. Mike stated how Stacey had this customer "wrapped around her finger", in large due to how attractive she was. He told her she would likely go far in the organization because "we like to further those who make the best overall impression on the customer." Stacey notes that Mike was happily married and displayed no sexual advance towards her, but seemed to value her attractiveness as a valuable (organizational) asset. She was also told that Mr. Matthers (Mike's Boss) held this view as well.

Is this an isolated story of workplace appearance discrimination? Probably not. The thought process behind this revelation may, in fact, be commonplace. The behavior and actions displayed by many bosses we observed were consistent with "Mike's" explicit comments.

Carefully recording any written records or explicit statements regarding workplace appearance attitude is the first step in combating workplace appearance discrimination. If you are unable to access written records or collect statements, some simple statistics should be collected to ascertain the "workplace beauty level."

b) APPEARANCE STATISTICS

The second method for determining whether your workplace is sensitive to (your) appearance is to employ a very basic statistical analysis. If you agree that 10 out of 100 equals 10%, you can perform this analysis. By following the guidelines in section E, and answering questions 1-4 as they apply to your workplace, you can easily determine how sensitive your workplace is to your appearance. For example, if you determine from question #1 that most upper-level managers are equal to or above Appearance Quotient #2, then appearance is an unwritten qualification for joining your workplace's upper echelon. We asked a group of people working at a local hospital to rank their upper management in terms of attractiveness. The following distribution was agreed upon by the entire group of 5 for upper management in this hospital (please note that doctors not in administrative positions were excluded from this survey).

STATISTICAL APPEARANCE DISTRIBUTION OF HOSPITAL ADMINIS-TRATORS AND MANAGEMENT (excluding staff doctors)

CATEGORY	*Percent (%)*
Category 1 (Beautiful)	01%
Category 2 (Very Attractive)	68%
Category 3 (Average)	29%
Category 4 (Somewhat Unattractive)	02%
Category 5 (Very Unattractive)	00%

This same group then rated the entire hospital staff from photographs provided whereby the following distribution evolved:

STATISTICAL APPEARANCE DISTRIBUTION OF ALL HOSPITAL WORKERS

CATEGORY	*Percent (%)*
Category 1 (Beautiful)	02%
Category 2 (Very Attractive)	18%
Category 3 (Average)	70%
Category 4 (Somewhat Unattractive)	07%
Category 5 (Very Unattractive)	03%

This simple exercise reveals some rather astonishing findings. If we compare the statistical distribution of top hospital administrators to the distribution of the entire hospital staff, we see a disproportionate number of attractive persons in upper management than on the general staff. By employing the following formula to these findings, we can determine the hospital's appearance "sensitivity factor."

Appearance Sensitivity = [percent of category 1's + percent of category 2'S (in administration only)]/ [percent of category 1'S + percent of category 2'S (on total staff)]

The numbers (Appearance Sensitivity) would be:

$$(1\% + 68\%) / (2\% + 18\%) = 69\% / 20\% = 3.45$$

The quotient of 3.45 means that if you are very attractive or beautiful, you're 3.45 times more likely to obtain an administrator or senior level management position than someone equally qualified but less attractive!

This same method can be employed for questions 2-4 in section E. Simply substitute the words "ADMINISTRATOR" with "HIRED PERSONS", "PROMOTED PERSONS" and "FIRED/LAID-OFF PERSON" to determine the appearance sensitivity for those actions at your workplace. Try this exercise and determine the appearance sensitivity factor for your place of work. Any number above 1 means that your workplace is likely to hire and promote persons based largely on their appearance. If the number is less than or equal to 1, then your workplace does not generally discriminate based on appearance. For persons laid-off or fired, just replace the Category 1's & 2's with Category 4's and 5's in both equations to determine if unattractive persons are being let go at a higher rate than attractive persons. While the realities of these findings may be sobering, be careful about discussing the statistics about your workplace unless you are in an environment which is open (receptive) to revelations of this nature. Such a disclosure is strongly discouraged unless your management fully accepts the concepts presented herein.

The determination of appearance sensitivity for your workplace can be invaluable if you feel you've been unjustly passed over for promotion based on appearance or fired/laid off due to your appearance, or not hired in favor of someone more attractive. The sensitivity number can help defend your position if you decide to pursue appearance discrimination charges.

2. COMBATING & OVERCOMING WORKPLACE APPEARANCE DISCRIMINATION

If you believe that appearance discrimination is being practiced at your workplace, your next question may be "How can I fight back?" or, "How can I combat it (appearance discrimination)?" or, "How can I best combat appearance discrimination without jeopardizing my career?." We'll look at various methods for combating workplace appearance discrimination from the least to most effective based on research and personal experiences. The approaches vary widely and depend on factors including collected evidence, your personality, your aversion to (or willingness to take) risk, and co-worker support. Let's first examine the least effective method for combating appearance discrimination.

a) APPEARANCE DISCRIMINATION LAW SUITS

Success in filing an appearance discrimination law suit is heavily dependent on the following factors being true in order of relative priority:

1. Your career has been directly adversely affected by the practice of appearance discrimination.

2. You have written evidence of superiors practicing appearance discrimination.

3. You possess evidence of verbal comments made by superiors related to appearance discrimination which can be corroborated in a court of law.

4. You are strong-willed, will not be intimidated, and will persist in proceeding with the suit regardless of likely defense attacks against your character, etc. in court.

5. You are not worried about negative co-worker reaction, possible superiors' back-lashes, poor work assignments, or other potential harassment (even termination) if you remain with the same company.

Since most people lack sufficient evidence under items #2 and #3 above, appearance discrimination lawsuits are filed much less frequently than other discrimination suits (i.e. race, age, etc.). However, the rate at which appearance discrimination lawsuits are being filed is rising. Some municipalities have even passed laws against appearance discrimination. In 1992, Santa Cruz, California passed a city ordinance against appearance discrimination. This ordinance is under consideration for passage by other municipalities across the country.

An appearance discrimination lawsuit should only be used as a last resort. The process of going through any sort of lawsuit is long, grueling, and expensive. The filer typically becomes the subject of character assassination attacks which can understandably upset one's psychological well-being. It might be best to file an appearance discrimination lawsuit after you have left your (accused) company in order to avoid the likely in-plant retribution. If considering filing an appearance discrimination lawsuit, consult a competent attorney. A appearance discrimination lawsuit should only be considered after other courses of action have been exhausted.

b) BLOWING THE WHISTLE TO UPPER MANAGEMENT:

Another (somewhat ineffective) approach toward combating appearance discrimination is to make upper management or Human Resource officials aware of it. However, similar to lawsuits, this approach requires solid evidence that the charged behavior is actually occurring. If you do not have solid evidence, it is strongly advised that you not approach upper management. Also, you must know the management relationships within your business. You'll want to consider another approach if upper management is either closely tied to, or holds in high regard, the accused individual. Backlash from management against you for "blowing the whistle" can be expected if one or more of the following holds true:

1. The accused person is critical to (your) business' success;

2. Upper management persons are friends with the accused;

3. Your evidence is weak, subjective, and solely based on (your) personal observations or conversations;

4. Management has a less than ethical reputation, or discourages open communication and tends to operate "behind closed doors", issuing edicts to the working masses.

If you suspect backlash from management, then your management is not very open and would be unlikely to change their appearance discrimination behavior (or even admit that it exists). You may want to consider another, more effective, approach.

c) EDUCATING THE DISCRIMINATOR(S):

A more effective approach to combating appearance discrimination is to "sensitize" the persons practicing it. Since judging a person's appearance is largely a subconscious process, many persons often practice appearance discrimination without being aware of their actions. People who practice workplace appearance discrimination merely continue to practice behavior which they follow outside the organization where, although it may be somewhat more common, it remains inappropriate. Seldom will anyone correct this behavior outside the workplace, and it typically continues as part of this person's "acceptable" behavior. If no one educates these people about their inappropriate behavior outside the workplace, then it likely follows them into the workplace. It is then up to you, if you want this behavior to cease, to educate the one practicing appearance discrimination that it is wrong!

There are many ways to educate and sensitize people that appearance discrimination is inappropriate. The amount, and directness, of education will directly depend on the expected reaction and ramifications from the person you're attempting to educate. If that person is your boss and he or she is expected to react negatively, then a subtle, long-term, or even anonymous approach may be appropriate. If the person/boss is open, and has limited recourse over your "destiny" (i.e. you report to other bosses as well), then a more open and aggressive education process may be in order. The choice of approach and rate of education depends largely on your knowledge of the situation and should be adjusted as the education process evolves. Some methods for educating the appearance discriminator are as follows (from least to most aggressive):

METHODS FOR EDUCATING A WORKPLACE
APPEARANCE DISCRIMINATOR

1. Anonymously mailing this book or applicable sections/rules from this book;
2. Writing an anonymous letter;
3. Making subtle comments/remarks;
4. Having a casual talk about your feeling/perceptions of office atmosphere OR "other people's" perceptions and displeasure;
5. Having a serious talk about your displeasure with the situation;
6. Writing a signed letter noting your displeasure with the situation;
7. Noting or questioning the behavior while it happens.

d) CONFORMING TO THE ORGANIZATION/SITUATION

A more effective method for overcoming workplace appearance discrimination is to conform to, or exceed, the appearance standards set forth by management. If possible, change your appearance to be more professional, more presentable, even more appealing by "beating these discriminatory persons at their own game!" While never giving up and ignoring the appearance discrimination that is occurring, you are better able to advance the cause of appearance fairness than someone viewed as a "malcontent, "boat rocker," or "adversary." The best way to work within the confines of your workplace is to work within the informal and formal appearance rules established for success. This approach requires "swallowing" a bit of pride by "giving in", but is easier to implement and may lead you to greater success over the long run. Perhaps the best way to succeed is to follow appearance rule #23.

Appearance Rule #23
(workplace)

"YOU should act, dress, and generally appear like the person in the position you desire to obtain without compromising YOUR integrity or ethical standards."

The proofs for appearance rule #23 are:

1. Would you expect bosses to promote someone very like, or someone radically different from themselves, in terms of dress, actions, mode of operating, etc.? Imitation is the best form of flattery and this certainly holds true in the business world. People tend to get along with others who appear like themselves. Apply this to your workplace and reap the rewards.

2. Ever hear the term, "management clones?" This term is used in large companies to depict the homogenous management in terms of their dress, appearance, problem-solving approaches, etc.. If you seek such a (management) position, better start "cloning" yourself and (appear to) be part of the "in" crowd.

Appearance rule #23 simply means that if the organization found the person currently in the position you desire to be acceptable and presentable, then they would more easily perceive you in that position if you looked and acted like him/her. The organization is sending an unwritten message about the type of person they want in each of these positions. Bosses also tend to be most comfortable with people who look and act like themselves. Managers have been found to be more likely to promote others who are very similar to themselves and who uphold their own "approved" behavior method(s). By modeling yourself after your boss or boss's boss (if you respect and admire them), you'll more likely move forward/upward in the organization as "acceptable" or "desirable." Of course you wouldn't want to model some behavior that was unacceptable to your own ethical standards or change yourself so radically as to lose your identity. Joining or acquiescing is simply a method which can be used for people who want to get ahead and further their careers rather than fight the system by "righting" appearance discrimination injustices. Depending on the degree of appearance discrimination occurring in your workplace, changing your appearance might not be enough. If your boss is only hiring/promoting young blond females, and you are older and less attractive, you might want to consider leaving the organization for one that values productivity versus "attractiveness!"

e) LEAVING FOR A LESS APPEARANCE SENSITIVE ORGANIZATION

If all else fails in terms of education, bringing the matter to management's attention, and changing your appearance is either out of the question or has not worked, then you might consider leaving your current place of employment. Compare your values and appearance standards to those of your current employer and determine whether the appearance related actions of your employer violate your own moral, ethical, or spiritual beliefs. If in violation, and reasonable attempts to change things have failed, then we advise leaving your current employer for one whose (appearance) values more closely resemble your own.

CHAPTER 3 SUMMARY

A. Research has shown that attractive persons, on the average, earn 12% more than unattractive persons.

B. Occupations that deal with the public and influencing others often require a person to be attractive.

C. Appearance is less relevant in occupations where people are not required to deal with the public.

D. Some organizations have a "glass ceiling" for promotion, where only attractive persons are selected for upper management from the ranks of the (otherwise) equally qualified.

E. Research has shown attractive persons to be more effective at the art of persuasion.

F. Attractive persons are assumed to possess more organizationally desirable traits than unattractive persons.

G. Attractive persons are assumed to have greater ability to perform a given task than an unattractive person.

H. Management determines how important appearance is to the organization and whether appearance discrimination will occur.

I. Immature, less educated, or autonomous managers are more likely to practice appearance discrimination.

J. The more a manager is consumed by his or her own appearance, the more likely he or she will be concerned with your appearance.

K. Determining whether appearance discrimination exists at your workplace involves obtaining written records, recording verbal comments, and determining, via statistical data, your workplace "appearance sensitivity factor."

L. A workplace appearance sensitivity factor greater than "1" means your organization may practice appearance discrimination.

M. Appearance discrimination lawsuits, while increasing in number, are difficult to win without solid evidence.

N. Informing upper management of ongoing appearance discrimination may cause backlash against you and injure your long-term career prospects with that employer.

O. Educating the person committing appearance discrimination may help alleviate the situation.

P. Conforming to or exceeding your organization's "appearance code" will enhance your chance for success within that organization.

Q. Mimicking the appearance (dress, style) of your boss(es) will enhance your chances to be looked upon more favorably for promotion, retainment, raises, etc..

R. You may want to leave your current employer if your appearance values are incompatible with those set by your employer.

CHAPTER
4

HOW APPEARANCE EFFECTS YOUR ABILITY TO ACHIEVE WEALTH, GAIN POWER, AND ACHIEVE SUCCESS

Ever notice that wealthy persons tend to be attractive? Or have you ever taken notice of the number of very attractive people in shopping malls, walking around town, or driving along the highway? We made some startling discoveries while researching for this book on the direct connection between the ability to obtain wealth and power and a person's attractiveness. This chapter tells you where you stand in terms of being successful and gaining wealth and power. Your appearance is key to your success and can virtually wreak havoc with your attempts to succeed if you choose to ignore this critical component to "getting ahead."

As stated in Chapter 3, research has found that attractive persons earn, on the average, 12% more than unattractive persons. Also, remember the CEO study which found 87% of CEO's rated as very attractive or beautiful, or the research which conclusively proved that attractive people have greater ability to effectively influence others than do unattractive persons? What does all this mean in terms of your ability to gain wealth and power? This chapter is dedicated to revealing the answers to this most perplexing and elusive question.

A. What comes first—wealth or attractiveness?

One question we asked regarding the attractive and the wealthy, like the chicken and the egg, is what came first? Was it that wealthy people had greater access to appearance-enhancing resources which made them look more attractive? Or was it that attractive people had greater ability to accumulate wealth? So, the two questions are:

1. Is wealth a pre-existing condition allowing one to further enhance their appearance to become attractive? (or)

2. Is an attractive appearance a "ticket" to achieving wealth?

Evidence and research alike seem to indicate the answer is "yes" to both questions.

The answer to the first question is yes, due to research and evidence we uncovered which prove attractive people consistently had more opportunities to gain greater wealth and achieve success than do unattractive people. We likened this phenomenon to an elitist club seeking new members. Those who are attractive are given greater opportunity and more readily allowed to join the affluent "club." We'll cover in detail just how and why the attractive have this imperceptible advantage in life in Sections C through E.

The answer to the second question is also yes because more appearance-enhancement opportunities present themselves for the wealthy than for the less financially fortunate. Those who have accumulated wealth have the (monetary) assets to capitalize on a far greater array of appearance-enhancement services and facilities than do the non-wealthy. Those who achieve this wealthy status have access to an array of assets to further improve their appearance, and typically become more attractive, which is a proven component to becoming successful. This self-maintaining attractiveness phenomenon is covered in Section B.

B. BEING WEALTHY FACILITATES AN ATTRACTIVE APPEARANCE

Being wealthy makes it much easier to maintain an enhanced appearance. Many things one can do to improve their appearance (which will be covered in detail in chapter 7) cost money. The more money you have available, the easier (and more feasible) it is to obtain these appearance-enhancing procedures/products. Professional hair styling, professional cosmetic application, personal health/fitness trainer, dietitian, access to health clubs, cosmetic surgery, or the ability to purchase expensive exercise machines for in home use, are more accessible if one has ample financial resources. Persons who have attained wealth (for any reason) have greater access to maintain and enhance their appearance, if they so choose. Take, for example, wealthy movie stars and entertainment personalities. They have access to, and typically maintain, personal health trainers, makeup artists, world-renowned professional hair stylists, complete gyms and Olympic-size swimming pools in their homes, and even have personal dietitians. These people are rich largely due to their appeal on the screen and stage. Once at the top, they maintain their success by utilizing their wealth for appearance enhancement and maintenance. This cycle of wealth attainment and appearance enhancement keeps their success from being prematurely "derailed." The same goes for other successful persons. Once realizing the wealth, their appearance is more easily maintained and therefore, provides the potential for future success or maintenance of their current position.

Appearance Rule #24

Persons of greater financial means generally have greater opportunity to attain an attractive appearance since they have easier access to appearance enhancement equipment, facilities, experts, and services. Persons of lesser financial means generally have fewer opportunities to improve their appearance and must apply extra effort and personal conviction to overcome their lack of access, etc.

Proofs for Appearance Rule #24 are as follows:

1. Who is most likely to have any of the following appearance enhancements at their disposal, someone of means or one short of ready cash?
   a) Professional Weight Trainer

b) Nutrition Specialist
c) Professional Hair Stylist
d) Makeup Consultant
e) Clothes Consultant
f) Health Club or Spa Membership
g) Personal Weight Training Equipment at home
h) Stair-Stepping or Bicycling equipment at home
I) Expensive Clothes
J) Manicurist

Is it likely that this person would be one "of means" or one that is "short" on cash? Maybe a person with limited funds can swing a few of these, but their access is surely limited.

2. A family stretches to make ends meet and the parents must work long hours to stay afloat. Most of their available time is devoted to maintaining the family. How much time, if any, will these people devote to appearance-enhancing activities?

While it is true that persons of greater means have greater opportunities to enhance their appearance, it is only an opportunity. A person must be intelligent enough to understand the link between appearance-enhancement and the greater opportunity to succeed in life. This is highly dependent on upbringing and what influence your parents had. If you were taught that your appearance counts either by keeping trim, working out, or dressing nice, then you'll probably follow these teachings as an adult, if only to the extent of your means unless you apply extra effort for the lack of means.

Unattractive persons are subject to the same, yet opposite (negative), cycle. These persons have less chance to enhance their appearance, primarily due to lack of wealth. If they also maintain a poor appearance, they stand a poorer chance of obtaining wealth.

C. HOW AN ATTRACTIVE APPEARANCE LEADS TO HIGHER SELF-ESTEEM AND ULTIMATELY TO GREATER SUCCESS

Attractive people are often the center of attention and receive much positive (verbal and non-verbal) feedback regarding their appearance. People often attempt to befriend them, look at them, make positive comments on their appearance, etc.. This sustained positive treatment of attractive persons by other members of society, enhances their mental image and enforces the notion that they are:

1) VALUABLE
2) DESIRABLE
3) SOUGHT-AFTER
4) IN-DEMAND
5) AESTHETICALLY PLEASING
6) FUN TO BE AROUND
7) SOCIALLY ACCEPTABLE

APPEARANCE IS EVERYTHING

Society continually reinforces these positive mental attributes via continued positive treatment. The cyclic maintenance of a positive self-image for attractive people is the end-result of society's treatment. Much research has been done in this area proving that attractive persons gain higher self-esteem than do unattractive persons. Although much is common sense, it is no less astonishing.

1. In 1967, researcher Kurtzberg, et. al. reported that New York jail inmates with abnormal physical traits (e.g. hump nose, protruding ears, tattoos, conspicuous facial scars, or needle tracks) lacked a sense of self-worth and believed that their physical appearance stereotyped them as "boisterous", "mean", "aggressive", "immature", "low in intelligence", and "addicted to violence."

2. In 1983, researchers Adams and Read found that high levels of facial attractiveness in undergraduate students were associated with more frequent interaction attempts than with people of medium or low facial attractiveness, and that attractive people were more likely to internalize the view that they are highly socially skilled. They also reported that unattractive female undergraduates were less likely to engage in frequent interaction attempts than their attractive peers. Also, they were likely to use less desirable interaction styles, including elements such as being demanding, interruptive, opinionated, submissive, or antagonistic.

The above research led us to formulate Appearance Rule #25 which directly illustrates the connection between being attractive and being self-confident.

Appearance Rule #25

Since attractive persons ARE GENERALLY treated more favorably, they tend to develop high levels of self esteem and self-confidence which, in turn, provide greater potential for success.

Proofs for Appearance Rule #25 are:

1. How would you feel if every time you want out you were greeted with smiles, people who wanted to meet and befriend you, and were always telling you that you "looked great, beautiful, gorgeous", "were a hunk", etc.? Would you feel bad and want to "cower in the corner?" What would such treatment do to your self-confidence?

2. You find it easy to get a date with another man or woman and are often asked out or flirted with by the opposite sex. Would you worry about your appearance or feel pretty good about it? Would you feel that you can find dates "at any time," that your spouse "is fortunate and better treat you right", and that you are a pretty "hot commodity?"

3. Whom would you expect to excel in life, the self-confident, outgoing, always friendly person, or the shy, introverted, person? If you picked the self-confident person, you likely also picked the more attractive one!

This is why many attractive people are viewed as socially adept and are typically extroverts. Since they receive so much positive attention, there is little reason for them to retreat or be shy, even from a possible negative encounter with another person. Attractive people are simply used to being treated in a nice, friendly, receptive manner.

On the other side of the coin, unattractive people often go unnoticed or greeted by a cool reception. Researchers Krebs and Adinolfi (p. 19) stated it as follows:

> "The low incidence of dating for the physically unattractive has been interpreted as rejection by the opposite sex. In order to be actively rejected, one must be noticed; but the present data suggest that the physically unattractive tend to be ignored. It may be less that the unattractive make a bad impression and more that they do not make an impression at all."

Also, renowned researchers Rumsey and Bull stated in 1986:

> "that if facially disfigured people attempt to engage others in brief encounters in the street, many members of the public will try to avoid them if possible, by increasing their pace, averting their gaze, and attempting to ignore the presence of the disfigured person (in much the same way as many of us try to avoid market researchers, opinion pollsters, etc.). This avoidance is picked up by the disfigured person, who frequently interprets it as a form of rejection."

Findings from other studies also indicate that attractive people tend to greet the facially unattractive in a cool, avoiding manner. The types of reactions toward the unattractive we read about while researching this book were far-reaching and varied. These reactions included the following:

1) PHYSICALLY AVOIDED CONTACT
2) SHORTER INTERACTIONS
3) LARGER PERSONAL SPACE PROVIDED THAN FOR ATTRACTIVE PERSONS
4) MET UNATTRACTIVE WITH FROWNS OR BLANK STARES
5) RELUCTANTLY OFFERED A HANDSHAKE
6) SHORT, CURT GREETINGS SUCH AS "OH, HI"

7) AVOIDED EYE CONTACT
8) VERBALLY ABUSED IN SOME FORM
9) STATEMENTS OF ASSUMED INCOMPETENCE, POOR ACCOMPLISH-
    MENTS, LAZINESS (MOSTLY DIRECTED TOWARD OVERWEIGHT PER-
    SONS), AND GENERAL LACK OF INTELLECTUAL CAPABILITY

Reactions such as these tend to support low self-esteem by the unattractive who are treated in this manner. Sustained negative treatment of unattractive persons by society, generally tends to lessen their self-esteem and inhibit self-confidence. The (types of) messages being sent tend to build a negative mental image of themselves and enforces the notion that they are:

1) FLAWED
2) UNDESIRABLE
3) SOCIALLY UNACCEPTABLE
4) NOT VALUED
5) AESTHETICALLY DISPLEASING
6) REPULSIVE
7) UNEXCITING
8) UNFRIENDLY/ANTI-SOCIAL
9) UNRESPONSIVE

The research above led us to formulate Appearance Rule #26, which illustrates the connection between being unattractive and having low self-confidence (esteem).

Appearance Rule #26

Since unattractive persons ARE GENERALLY treated less favorably, they tend to develop lower levels of self-esteem and self-confidence which detract from their chance to succeed (converse of rule #25).

Proofs for Appearance Rule #26:

1. How would you feel if, every time you went out, people tended to avoid you or were generally unfriendly toward you? Would you feel bad about yourself and want to "cower in the corner?" Would you wonder if something was wrong with you? Would your self-confidence be low or high? I know mine would be pretty low unless I did something to make up for it.

2. You find it difficult to get a date with another man or woman and are often rejected when asking others out or infrequently asked out yourself. Would you worry about your appearance or feel pretty good about it? Maybe this is does not pertain to you, but surely you can see how another might feel less than good about themselves in this situation. Just put yourself "in their shoes!"

3. How do you feel when you are out with an attractive person in a social setting and they receive disproportionately more attention than you? The other person is being "hit on" more, talked to more, smiled at more, and seems generally to be the center of attention while you are being mildly greeted or ignored completely. I've been in this situation more times than I care to count, and have felt just awful, even angry, and wondering exactly "what is wrong with me?"

Researchers Secord & Jourard in 1953 found that women with eating disorders have extremely low self-esteem, feelings of being a "bad" person, and abnormal fear of rejection or total abandonment. Our research also found that unattractive persons are very often excluded from certain social circles, conversations, employment/promotional opportunities, making friends, dating, marrying, mating, and having children.

That is the reason some unattractive people are viewed as ANTI-social and typically appear as introverts. Since they receive so much negative treatment, they retreat, become very shy, or coy due to a (perceived) possible negative encounter with another person. Unattractive people are used to being greeted in a cool, unfriendly, and unreceptive manner. Such continued negative treatment naturally leads to lower self-esteem and self-confidence.

What does all this have to do with being successful and obtaining wealth? Robert L. Schuyler, who authored "The Power of Positive Thinking," wrote "There are two types of people in the world, those who think they can and those who think they can't. In fact, both types are right, depending on the individual!!!"

Countless others have written on the power of positive mind thoughts, believing in yourself, and having a "can do" attitude. These authors, along with other researchers, concluded that there is a high correlation between success in life and a strong sense of self-confidence/high self-esteem. The power associated with positive thinking and believing you have value to add society plays a large role in providing the motivation necessary to do something about it and putting action plans in place to accomplish something. Without strong belief in your self-worth or a high degree of self-confidence, overall success and enhanced wealth tend to be elusive.

As we've seen, the experience of the attractive in meeting others tends to be a very positive and mentally fulfilling experience, thus leading to a valuable, positive self-image. Higher levels of self-confidence and self-esteem often result from consistent positive treatment! This higher self-confidence also leads to higher levels of drive, ambition, and perseverance, all crucial components in the Life Success Formula (refer to Section F of this chapter).

Unattractive persons, on the other hand, are often withdrawn from society, feel poorly about themselves, and consistently have lower levels of self-esteem and self-confidence than attractive persons. These (less attractive) persons often feel they have little value as members of society.

Basically stated, attractive persons, via their treatment by others, are generally provided greater opportunity to develop higher self-esteem and self-confidence than are unattractive persons. This higher self-confidence and self-esteem, in turn, provides greater opportunity for success and accumulation of wealth. While self-esteem and self-confidence are only one component to the Life Success Formula, they provide a component advantage over those not possessing these characteristics. There are indeed numerous examples of the unattractive succeeding in life and having immense self-confidence. These cases truly illustrate that overall success is multi-dimensional and dependent on many factors as will be pointed out in Section F. An unattractive person may be very intelligent, highly educated, have overcome obstacles and persisted in developing smooth social skills despite early (in life) poor treatment by others. Opportunities are either viewed as being provided by others (regardless of poor or good treatment), or as being available for the taking (I will succeed no matter what people say!). Unattractive, successful people have a view that opportunities are for the taking, not accepting or internalizing the treatment of others and letting that negatively effect their self-esteem or self-confidence.

D. ATTRACTIVENESS AND THE EFFECT ON THE OPPORTUNITY TO EFFECTIVELY "NETWORK"

As we learned in Section C, attractive people are treated more favorably than the unattractive and provided greater opportunities to develop self-confidence, self-esteem, and socialize. These people are widely sought after to befriend, date or possibly marry. Unattractive persons, on the other hand, tend to retreat and develop low self-esteem based on previous poorer treatment received from others. As the old adage states, "practice makes perfect", and the attractive are provided many more opportunities to sharpen (develop) their social skills by meeting new people. The unattractive are consistently provided fewer socialization opportunities and typically tend to appear awkward in the presence of others (due to the somewhat cooler reception they receive). Remember the research from Section C which read that:

> "attractive people were more likely to internalize
> the view that they are highly socially skilled and
> that unattractive female undergraduates were less
> likely to engage in frequent interaction (with an-
> other) attempts"

Since the ability to network in business is critical in finding a new job, finding new opportunities, and learning about the competition, being attractive is certainly an advantage. Given that two persons have the same motivation, intelligence, exposure opportunities, etc., the attractive person has a distinct advantage over the unattractive person due to increased numbers of, and more qualitative, encounters with others. Appearance Rule #27 deals with this phenomenon.

Appearance Rule #27

Attractive persons ARE GENERALLY provided more opportunities to socialize and make friends than unattractive persons of similar capabilities. Therefore, the attractive have greater opportunities to succeed regardless of the endeavor.

Proofs for Appearance Rule #27 are:

1. Who would you expect to get a job after being laid-off? A person who is shy, has few contacts/friends, and is generally withdrawn or one who is friendly, attractive, and outgoing?

2. Who would you expect to be elected to be President of your Chamber of Commerce? Somebody introverted and withdrawn, or somebody very outgoing, personable, and whom has many business friends and social contacts? Would this person likely be attractive or unattractive?

Real life example of Appearance Rule #27:

Bill and Mike started a service business in Philadelphia. They both were committed to the success of this business and both intelligent, educated, motivated, and of similar financial means. However, Bill was much more attractive (Category #2) than Mike (Category #4). Bill was somehow much better (adept) in making business contacts, had many more dates than Mike, and became the person customers requested when calling on the business. Mike seemed to prefer it this way and was more comfortable performing technical tasks (accounting, process, taxes, etc.). Later on, Mike and Bill had a falling out about Mike's perception that Bill was trying to dominate the business decisions. They decided to dissolve their partnership and formed two independent companies from the one.

Bill hired a technical consultant to perform the duties that Mike had usually performed. Mike hire a technical consultant as well and decided to perform the selling and customer interfacing himself. A large opportunity emerged to provide services to a major Philadelphia area business which could significantly increase the size and profitability of either business. Bill learned about this opportunity from a former customer, bid on the job, won the contract, and now has a thriving, flourishing business. Mike, on the other hand, never heard of this opportunity and eventually went out of business, in large because he never had the opportunity to develop an extensive business network like Bill! Though Mike was equally capable as Bill, he lacked the "easiness" with people that Bill possessed. Mike told me that "Bill was always in the limelight. People always wanted to talk and befriend him. He had that knack of getting along with people. People just gravitated to him over me." I asked if he thought whether Bill's attractiveness had anything to do with that situation. Mike said "Oh, definitely! Bill always got the breaks because he was a looker."

This situation illustrates one instance where an attractive person was provided greater opportunity to meet others and develop a network. There are countless other examples where the attractive person has/had a distinct advantage over the unattractive person. Like self-esteem and self-confidence, the ability to network is part of the Life Success Formula (see section F). Just another advantage provided to attractive over unattractive people. Attractive people typically utilize this advantage and the unattractive must generally work harder to overcome this disadvantage.

E. PROVE THE WEALTH/APPEARANCE CONNECTION FOR YOUR-SELF

As we researched this book, we became very aware of people we encountered. We noticed of their appearance category (AQ), what they wore, how they handled themselves, their physical makeup, and other appearance-related factors. We made some startling discoveries that we'll share with you. The following correlation exercise is both intriguing and fun and may help you prove what we have been talking about in terms of the relationship between wealth and appearance.

When we were doing interviews and research for Chapter 2 (Relationships and Appearance), we found a most interesting correlation associated with very attractive couples and noted some characteristics of their appearance. We found some items that were somewhat consistent, and others that were inconsistent. However, one factor was almost universally true. We call it our "ONE CARAT GUARANTEE." This is beyond an Appearance Rule, and we are willing to call it a "guarantee." I noticed more closely the females (being a male myself), and found an uncanny correlation between the female's attractiveness (AQ) and the size of her diamond ring. The more attractive the female was, the larger her diamond ring was. Very beautiful women usually wore diamond rings that were 1 carat or larger in total carat weight. Very attractive women also wore consistently larger diamond rings than their less attractive counterparts. We call this Appearance Rule #28.

Appearance Rule #28
(One Carat Guarantee)

Very beautiful women who wear diamond rings WILL ALMOST ALWAYS wear larger diamonds (1 carat+) than will less attractive women who also wear diamond rings.

Self-Proofs for Appearance Rule #28 are:

1. Next time you're out, take notice of the attractive females you encounter. Get a good look at the size of the diamond ring(s) they wear. Gauge the size based on your own experience. I'll bet the size of the rings you will find are exceptionally large, and much larger than ones you see displayed by less attractive women!

2. If so inclined, keep a little chart which maps the Appearance Quotient on the right (vertical) axis to the size (small, medium, large, and huge) of the diamond rings found worn by different women on the bottom (horizontal) axis. We did this at a holiday party and the results are found in Chart 4. Notice how most women ended up in the top, right of the chart, meaning that the most beautiful women had the largest rings.

3. We asked jewelers if they saw any correlation after we suspected a connection. One jeweler said, "It's true, the beautiful women are treated the best and get the biggest rings." We asked why this might be. He said, "Wealthier men get the more beautiful women!"

We also noticed that very attractive people disproportionately drove the nicest automobiles, lived in the nicest homes, and wore the nicest clothes. Of course, not all attractive people are wealthy, nor all wealthy people attractive. Look at the richest men in America today. Some are attractive, yet others are unattractive. We simply mean that disproportionately, attractive people have more wealth and greater opportunity to accumulate such wealth. Again, it comes down to opportunity which everyone has access to. It is what you do with opportunity, not merely that it is provided, that determines success. That is why even unattractive people succeed—they seize opportunity! While more limited for the unattractive compared to the attractive, it (opportunity) still exists and is there "for the taking!"

Does this means that you must be self-confident AND attractive to accumulate wealth or are they only part of some larger equation? What is the key to success and what does it have to do with your appearance?

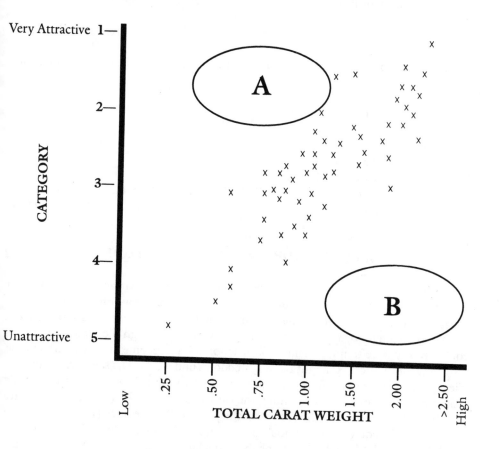

Relationship Between Attractiveness of Women &
Size of Diamond Rings Worn

Chart 4

F. BEING ATTRACTIVE IS AN ADVANTAGE TOWARD OBTAINING SUCCESS, BUT NO GUARANTEE

Ray Crock, the founder of McDonald's, once indicated, all people have an equal chance of making it America. I believe this statement is true and it relates, at least in part, to a person's appearance. Appearance is one part of the multi-faceted equation on what makes people successful and wealthy. The more parts of the equation you have going for you, the more likely you are to be successful in life. Appearance is one component which gets you in the door and helps you influence others. There are many more characteristics which make a person successful. The total value of a person and their chance for success in life is the sum total of these characteristics. We call this the Life Success Formula (LSF):

Success in Life is the effective utilization of the summation (adding together) of the components which comprise your personal capabilities as follows:

Success is the effective utilization of the: $SUM(A, I, E, D, AM, P, PS, PA, IN, H, SC)$

This formula basically says that success in life comes from the effective utilization of many components:

A	—	APPEARANCE
I	—	INTELLIGENCE
D	—	DRIVE
AM	—	AMBITION
P	—	PERSEVERANCE
PS	—	POLITICAL SAVVY (NETWORKING, ETC.)
PA	—	PERSONAL APPEAL (OPENNESS, FRIENDLINESS, ETC.)
IN	—	INTEGRITY
H	—	HONESTY
SC	—	SELF-CONFIDENCE (CAN DO ATTITUDE)

So we see that appearance plays a factor in the success equation as do many other factors. Depending on what you are trying to accomplish, the weight (importance) of appearance in the equation can change. For example, if you're trying to sell something, or get a modeling job, appearance (A), might be weighted high (i.e. 65%) in the total equation. If you're trying to land a construction job or become involved with church activities, appearance (A) might be weighted low (under 5%). The same weighting applies to the other success formula components. If you're trying to perform a simple task around the house like vacuuming the carpet, then all factors in the equation are zero (0), except Ambition (AM) to start the job and Perseverance (P) to get the job done. This job requires little or no Appearance, Intelligence, Political Savvy (unless a good show is on TV which needs to be shut off while the vacuuming is going on), etc. These factors do not play into the success equation for this task. So we see how important each factor is depends on the external situation and task to be accomplished.

There also exists different personal degrees of each success component, relating to your personal characteristics in each area. For example, you might be Very Attractive and rate your appearance as "high." Or you might be average and rate your appearance as "medium" in terms of a personal "score." Take a look at *Chart 5*. We rated the weight of each success component. For example, we felt that Drive (**D**), Perseverance (**P**), and Ambition (**AM**) were the most critical components to general success behind Intelligence (**I**) and Appearance (**A**). The numbers we assigned for this exercise are completely arbitrary and could be any numbers. As we stated before, the numbers will change based on the specific situation and task at hand. What is critical is how the numbers relate to each other in terms of relative priority for each specific situation.

Take for example the task of finding a date, having sex, and marrying in regard to appearance. In the beginning, the task requires appearance to be as high as possible. Most people are literally on their "best appearance behavior" when they are single and dating. They carefully watch their weight, work out, dress nicely, etc.. Once they have acquired a long-term partner, their appearance may continue to be important but probably less critical as when they were first dating. Since you passed the minimum "appearance entrance criteria" of your dating partner, you're now being rated on secondary personality qualities more than on your external appearance. Once marriage comes into play, many people gain weight, let themselves "go", and concentrate less on their appearance than when they were dating. They become "comfortable" in the thought that their mate no longer judges them on their appearance. Here we can see that, depending on the circumstance and task at hand, the Life Success Formula variables take on different importance (or weighting) factors. Some situations require appearance to rate high (getting certain public jobs, dating, selling, influencing, etc.), while other situations do not (gardening, construction, home improvement projects, visiting relatives, etc.). The same variability applies to the other Life Success Formula variables and should be taken into account when undertaking any task. The conscientious mapping of tasks to LSF variables will go a long way in determining your formula for success in life's objectives.

This is not to say that the unattractive cannot achieve the same levels of success, but research indicates that they have to work a degree harder if they are to realize the same levels of success. The *study conducted* in the fall of 1994, *highlighted* how much easier attractive people have it. Many instances of this fact were illustrated as follows:

A) *Tonya* and *Susan* were *women* set up to appear having run out of gas. *Susan* wore the same outfit as *Tonya*, but was much more attractive. *Tonya* waited 45 minutes before anyone would offer to assist (bring her gas). *Susan* had many cars "screeching" to a halt, many cars pulling over, and at least a dozen people stopped to help in a very short period of time. Six people actually ran to get *Susan* gas and her tank was over half-full in virtually no time at all. She (*Susan*) was offered all sorts of (gas) gifts from many people and worked far less harder than Michelle did to achieve the same result!

B) Mark and Mike's resumes were identically prepared with similar education and work experience. Mark was much more attractive than Mike. Mark was offered three out of three jobs, while Mike was offered none, even after preceding Mark at

APPEARANCE IS EVERYTHING

PERSONAL TRAITS	DEGREE		
	HIGH	MEDIUM	LOW
Appearance	50	25	5
Intelligence	80	40	0
Education	50	25	5
Drive, Ambition, Perserverance	80	40	0
Political Ability	50	25	5
Personal Appeal	40	20	5
Integrity	25	10	5
Honesty	25	10	5
self-Confidence	50	25	0

APPEARANCE HELPS BUT DOES NOT GUARANTEE SUCCESS IN LIFE!

Points	Success Potential
360-450	Very High
270-359	High
180-269	Moderate
90-179	Low
0-89	Very Low

Factors Which Effect Success
Chart 5

the same potential locations. Mike was told that they didn't have any room for him now. One interviewer said to another while interviewing Mark, "He looks like a stock broker." He was told, "You could be making $10,000 a month if you wanted." Another pair of *women* had a similar experience for totally different jobs. Diana was more attractive than Amy and was consistently offered jobs over Amy. In each case, the more attractive person was offered a chance at wealth and presented greater opportunity for getting ahead in life. Their attractiveness came first and allowed them the opportunity to join the attractive and wealthy elite (for much less effort than their equally qualified, less attractive counterparts).

These two situations illustrate that the attractive person consistently has an easier path to success. Had Michelle been more aggressive in flagging down cars and waved a white or red flag, or if she jumped up and down, she may have been more successful and more people may have gone to her aid. Also, if Mike had greater financial experience, some previous success in the financial markets, or some other edge (advantage), then he might have been just as successful as Mark. The point here is that Michelle and Mark had one component of the LSF that ensures success, wealth, power. etc.. Their attractive appearance mattered in the situations they dealt with and led to their success over their less attractive, yet equally qualified counterparts!

Appearance Rule #29

Attractive persons have a distinct advantage in obtaining success, wealth, power and advances in life over equally qualified, yet less attractive persons. These people have a higher rating in the life success formula and will likely be more successful, depending on their goals or tasks being attempted.

No self-proofs are needed for this rule. The *previous sections of this chapter* stand as testimonial for Appearance rule #29.

CHAPTER 4 SUMMARY

A. Attractive people earn, on average, 12% more than unattractive persons.
B. Most CEO's (over 87%) were rated as Very Attractive or Beautiful in an independent survey.
C. Attractiveness provides greater opportunity to be wealthy.
D. Wealth provides greater opportunity to be attractive.
E. The wealthy have many more attractive-enhancing opportunities at their disposal.
F. Attractive persons are treated more favorably by others and develop high levels of self-confidence and self-esteem.
G. Unattractive persons are treated less favorably by others and develop lower levels of self-confidence and self-esteem.
H. Attractive persons have an advantage in succeeding in life due to higher levels of self-esteem, self-confidence, and greater social capability.
I. Unattractive persons are at a disadvantage in succeeding in life due to lower levels of self-esteem, self-confidence, and lesser social capability.

e persons have a greater ability to build social and business networks than tive persons.

e persons have an advantage in succeeding in life due to their ability to build and utilize networks.

L. There is a high correlation between being attractive and being successful, but not 1-to-1.

M. Since there is not a 1-to-1 correlation between being attractive and being successful, unattractive people still have many opportunities to succeed.

N. A disproportionate number of attractive people live in the nicest homes, drive fancy cars, and wear the most expensive jewelry.

N. The wealthiest men attract the most beautiful women as mates.

O. Success in life is dependent on many factors in the Life Success Formula.

P. Appearance (**A**) is one factor which determines success and needs to be rated high to succeed in certain endeavors.

Q. The importance of any one variable in the Life Success Formula depends on the particular task at hand.

R. Unattractive persons need to work harder to accomplish the same tasks compared to attractive persons of similar capabilities.

CHAPTER
5

THE EFFECT OF GEOGRAPHIC REGION, AGE, EXPERIENCE, EDUCATION, AND INTELLIGENCE ON APPEARANCE DISCRIMINATION

While accurate in most cases, appearance discrimination rules are not necessarily universal. They are affected by certain external factors which determine the "trueness" of each rule or the degree to which a rule applies for a particular situation. These external factors are:

1. The **geographic region** in which one resides or originates
2. A person's **age and experience**
3. A person's **level of education/intelligence**
4. A person's **cultural background** and how they were raised (see Chapter 6, "Where does it all begin?")

These appearance discrimination "modifiers" determine the extent to which you may be discriminated against based on appearance and the importance of appearance to your particular situation. Keeping these factors in mind will significantly effect your ability to determine your course of action and predict the action of others regarding your appearance. Understanding these factors will help illuminate other variables in the appearance discrimination equation.

I. WHERE YOU LIVE DETERMINES THE IMPORTANCE OF YOUR APPEARANCE

Certain geographic areas are very sensitive to a person's appearance while others are almost totally oblivious to, even ignorant of, appearance in certain forms. Depending on where you live, the chance that you will be discriminated upon based on your appearance changes radically. We'll first look at areas where appearance is central to the life-style and then some areas where it is less important.

A. AREAS WHERE APPEARANCE IS A MAJOR FACTOR

1. METROPOLITAN AREAS:

When you think of the most glamorous people in the world, do you envision them living in a rural, farming region or a large city? Where would you go for the best make-up, best clothes, most glamorous restaurants? Obviously, many more opportunities exist in a metropolitan area to experience (and gain exposure to) appearance-related businesses. Likewise, there are many more layers of wealth, status, and power in metro-

than in smaller communities. A metropolitan area has many layers of af-
g from the lowly street person all the way up to the wealthiest and the
al.

What makes a metropolitan area more sensitive to appearance and its residents more likely to practice appearance discrimination? To find the answer, we must first look at the area's composition. A metropolitan area's multiple layers of class, status, power, and affluence are typically much deeper than you would find in a rural area. There are many classes of people in a metropolitan area ranging from some of the country's wealthiest to poorest. It is typically the upper layer of the most affluent and powerful that determine the appearance standard of any given area. Since a metropolitan area has more levels of affluence, the appearance standard is generally higher than in areas with fewer layers of affluence and power.

Appearance Rule #30

The greater the level of affluence in a given area, the MORE LIKELY that the appearance standard will be higher.

Proofs for Appearance Rule #30:

1) Would you expect an area with many wealthy people to generally be very unattractive (dress very sloppily, look unkempt, etc.) or would you expect them to look generally attractive (well-groomed, well-dressed, looking sharp)?

2) Would you expect the best dressed and well "heeled" people to live in a small, average income, farming community or a big city like New York, Paris, or London?

3) What would your first impression be when approaching a skyline on an interstate highway where the downtown area is full of beautiful, tall, modern buildings? Would you think the "upper crust of people" were affluent and sharp looking or poor and unkempt? How about if you approached a town with a few corn silos and generally small, older looking buildings?

Ironically, as in the third proof above, the layers of affluence for a given area are similar to that of the area's skyline. The more layers of affluence and class that a given area has, the more likely its skyline will be dominated by tall, modern and diverse buildings the more likely that this area has the affluence to economically support such structures when higher affluence levels exist, the more likely the area's appearance standard will be set higher.

Take New York or Chicago for example. Both skylines are comparably striking, distinct, tall, and diverse. Both metropolitan areas have many more affluence layers when compared to smaller communities. Small communities, in contrast, generally have very few class distinctions from poor to semi-affluent and their skylines are typically uniform, undistinguished, and rather commonplace.

Some of the world's richest people live within, nearby, or frequently visit, metropolitan areas. These people enjoy such appearance enhancement or reinforcing amenities as:

1) Exclusive nightclubs where people are very often only admitted if they look wealthy and/or beautiful. Oprah Winfrey conducted a study for a 1994 episode which highlighted just how the beautiful and affluent were treated better than those who are not. The show sent two men to an exclusive Beverly Hills nightclub wearing average clothes and driving an average vehicle. They were initially turned away by the door person saying "they were too crowded." The two men were then "whisked away" by show staff to a makeup studio, expensive clothes boutique, and sent back within 1 hour driving a fancy car. They gained entrance immediately! The crowd inside was the same size when they came back to the nightclub.

2) Fancy restaurants where ties, sport jackets, and (sometimes) formal wear, is required to enter. These are seldom found in smaller, rural areas.

3) Exclusive and expensive clothing salons where even the wealthy are excluded or ignored (if poorly dressed). Remember the movie "Pretty Woman" where Julia Roberts was ignored when she entered the salon wearing average looking clothes and was only waited on when the owners discovered she had money and wanted a "better appearance?"

4) Exclusive beauty salons where manicures and other beauty enhancement procedures can be more expensive than some peoples' entire weekly (or monthly) salary.

5) Private and exclusive health clubs offering private weight trainers, nutritionists and the finest equipment.

6) The best cosmetic surgeons money can buy.

7) Modeling agencies abound in such places as Beverly Hills, New York City, Chicago. You would seldom find these in a rural setting.

8) Television and commercial ad agencies that utilize "the look" to sell their clients' products and draw heavily from a close pool of models to help sell that "look." These agencies are more often found in large metropolitan areas.

9) Soap opera and TV studios are usually found in an area rich with models, affluent people, and an appearance enhancement industry to support their business. The common denominator to metropolitan areas is that the economies rely predominantly on service industries which, in turn, depend on the ability to influence people. These industries deal primarily with sales, legal, marketing, banking/brokering, management, public relations, etc.. Metropolitan areas are more in-

door and influence oriented than physically labor intensive. These industries rely on appearance to sell, manage, arbitrate, etc.. That is why metropolitan areas tend to value appearance and hold it in higher regard than do rural areas.

Appearance Rule #31

Areas whose economies rely on influence related industries (i.e. legal, sales, management, marketing, brokering, public relations, financial management, etc.) TEND TO maximize the importance of a person's appearance.

Proofs for Appearance Rule #31:

1. Would you expect persons working on Wall Street to be well dressed and attractive or generally unkempt and unattractive? What appearance standard do you think a typical Wall Street brokerage house maintains, low or high?

2. What would you expect to see upon entering the leading Public Relations firm in Chicago? Below average office accommodations and sloppy, unattractive people? Or would you expect such a firm to retain people who always put their "best face forward" and always appear sharp and professional?

While talking to others about this book, it was pointed out that the most powerful, influential, and attractive persons live in (or very near) large, metropolitan areas. These people include stock brokers, TV/motion picture executives, CEO's, super models, real estate barons, etc.. These people basically "own" the country, the most powerful, richest and most (no pun intended) famous. In the meantime, the "meek" live in the surrounding countryside. These people tend to be more humble, less wealthy or less attractive, and less powerful. A person surprisingly said to me while discussing this section, "That's what is meant by the statement 'The meek shall inherit the Earth."

If there is a nuclear conflict with another country, our cities, containing the most powerful and most beautiful people, will be gone, leaving only the 'meek' (from the farmlands and small towns) to inherit the Earth (or whatever's left). He went on to say that this was the way of returning the Earth to those not financially, physically, or personally motivated. The people controlling the food supply (meek, forgotten farmers) will then be in control of society!

While I am not particularly religious, I thought this statement intriguing enough to include. Draw your own conclusions. Just a thought provoking idea I thought you may find of interest.

2. AFFLUENT NON-METROPOLITAN AREAS

Areas apart from metropolitan areas can also maintain higher appearance standards. Small suburbs of smaller cities can be enclaves of the affluent such as an area close to my home in Syracuse, New York. The village of Skaneateles (pronounced

"Skinny-Atlas"), New York fits this situation. A small community of about 7,500 people, Skaneateles is a quaint village with many small specialty shops, well kept boutiques, Country Inns, fine restaurants, nice stores, and "neat as a pin" streets. The town overlooks a beautiful, spring-fed lake (same name as the town) that would rival the prettiest picture you can imagine. The town's residents include many affluent people. The people there, while surrounded by country (farmland), all tend to dress with expensive clothes, look well-groomed, and tend to be on the average, very attractive. While the few restaurants in town are more casual than you might find in a large, metropolitan area the typical dress includes expensive and stylish purses, sport coats, jackets, eyeglasses, slacks, shirts, etc.. Many people I've seen in this town are very attractive and tend to take good care of themselves. I tend to dress somewhat better than usual when dining out or even just visiting this town. Many affluent people from the northeastern United States visit Skaneateles in the Spring, Summer and Fall months and tend to "look the part" when coming to town. Most are well-dressed, well-groomed, and on average, look just as attractive as the town and its residents. It is as if they were attracted to this place by others of similar appearance and affluence. Appearance rule #32 directly applies to this situation.

Appearance Rule #32

Areas which encourage or maintain higher levels of affluence often encourage and maintain higher levels of personal appearance.

Proofs for Appearance Rule #32:

1. Where would you expect the most beautiful appearance people in the world to live, in a neighborhood nestled between factories and warehouses or some place like Beverly Hills, California or The Hamptons on Long Island?

2. Would you expect an area which encourages a person to achieve and accumulate wealth to encourage poor personal hygiene, sloppy dress standards, and generally not take care of one's body via exercise and proper diet, etc.?

Many other places come to mind including Newport, Rhode Island, Martha's Vineyard, Massachusetts, Carmel, California, Palm Beach, Florida, New Hope, Pennsylvania, Hilton Head, South Carolina, and Aspen, Colorado, where a higher appearance standard is set by the affluent community members. While not necessarily part of a metropolitan area like Chicago, New York or Los Angeles, these smaller areas attract and maintain people with higher appearance standards. Due to the higher level of amenities available, the quality of housing or area's natural beauty, these locations attract the attractive and affluent who prefer to live in less congestion and "hustle and bustle" away from large, metropolitan areas. Do you have one of these smaller but affluent areas in or near your community? Is it not a "magnet" for the attractive?

3. AREAS WHICH HAVE INDUSTRIES RELYING HEAVILY ON APPEARANCE

Some specific areas of the country rely on industries which, in turn, rely heavily on appearance. These areas are veritable magnets to those who are (or aspire to be) models, actors, makeup artists, hair stylists, etc.. Areas such as Hollywood, California and Orlando, Florida come readily to mind in this particular instance. These areas are dedicated to the entertainment industry which relies heavily on attractive actors, actresses, and the appearance-related occupations which support them. These areas are far more sensitive to a person's appearance than most other areas of the country.

In the March, 1995 issue of "Sassy" magazine, an article titled "Is it normal to hate beautiful girls?" appeared. This article talks about Los Angeles as "the beauty Mecca of the world." It goes on to say "Because the city (Los Angeles) is filled with "wanna-be" actresses and models working part-time jobs to survive, beautiful girls turn up wherever you go-as your bank teller, your school teacher and especially as your waitress, the profession of choice for most struggling starlets." The article talks about how the waitresses are all beautiful and not typical for an area. "Instead, at the local dive of a Winchell's, the woman handing me my glazed buttermilk is a svelte siren named Christabelle. Even on a bad hair day, Christabelle could double for Michelle Pfeiffer. No pocket of the city (L.A.), it seems, is beauty-free."

Hollywood and its surrounding areas abound with stories and instances similar to the one in Sassy magazine. "Tinsel town", as it is commonly called, attracts all that glitters, is beautiful, and appears to be attractive. How many people have not heard of Rodeo Drive in Beverly Hills, or Beverly Hills itself? The area boasts some of the world's most exclusive clothing boutiques, beauty salons, and jewelry stores. People who come from Beverly Hills are affluent and mostly attractive. There are tours to the stars' homes, tours along Rodeo Drive, and studio tours to see where the beautiful people congregate to influence and entertain us all.

The entire Beverly Hills area can be called a "Beauty Basin." The area and people it attracts tend to be beautiful or those who can make others look beautiful. This message is beamed to our homes, to our living rooms, to us as adults, and our children each and every day. It comes across in the form of commercials, talk shows, soap operas, sitcoms and yes, even news broadcasts. Ask yourself whether the beauty we see everyday is truly representative of America and the normal distribution of beauty. Do YOU look like these people? Does YOUR neighborhood contain many people that look like these people? Why then are television programs dominated by such unrepresentative beauties? What message are we sending to those who don't look as "perfect" or as "beautiful?" What effect does this have on our, and our children's, self-esteem? The answer to these questions can be found in Chapter 8.

4. OTHER AREAS WHERE APPEARANCE IS VALUED AS IMPORTANT

a. AREAS WHERE CULTURE ENCOURAGES WEALTH OR ACHIEVEMENT

Areas such the Hamptons on Long Island, NY, Northeastern New Jersey, and Westchester County, New York would be examples of areas where people strive to ac cumulate wealth and achieve success. Due to their proximity to New York City, there exists a largely competitive environment where the accumulation of wealth and career achievement is highly valued by many living there. Appearance, a very important part of one's ability to accumulate wealth and achieve in life, is valued and held to a higher standard.

b. AFFLUENT RESORT AREAS

Resort areas such as Lake Placid, New York, Boca Raton/Fort Lauderdale, Lake Tahoe, Long Beach Island, New Jersey, and Vail, Colorado all qualify as affluent resort areas where the appearance standard is set a notch higher than normal (casual). People who frequent these areas typically look their best and want to be seen looking their best.

c. MARINE TRAFFIC AREAS WHICH CATER TO YACHT OWNERS

Areas frequented by large yacht owners tend to cater to the rich, famous, and beautiful. Many private yacht clubs and marinas which cater to yachts in excess of 50' have (disproportionately) the most attractive people as owners and guests. Alexandria Bay and the surrounding Thousand Islands area of New York and Canada is one such area. Boasting many seasonal (summer) homes worth well over $1,000,000 and exclusive yacht clubs, the area abounds with people doing everything within their wealth-expanded power to look their best.

d. CERTAIN SOUTHERN STATES AS COMPARED TO NORTHERN STATES

Many people point out that appearance seems to be more of a concern with people living in certain southern states than it is in northern or Midwestern states. These people point to the strikingly beautiful women seen in Miss America Pageants hailing from states such as Texas, Kentucky, and Florida. Makeup, grooming, and dress tend to get more attention in general in certain southern states as compared to northern states. Why do you think that "Southern Belles", who are long known for their attractive beauty, receive such attention?

e. CALIFORNIA AS COMPARED TO THE REST OF THE WEST

Many models, health-conscious persons, actors, actresses, and fitness enthusiasts have gravitated to California, causing it to be known for many years as "the land of the beautiful." California, many people have said, has many more appearance-conscientious people than other parts of the West, and maybe in general, than the rest of the country (except perhaps New York City).

B. AREAS WHERE APPEARANCE IS LESS OF A FACTOR

1. RURAL AREAS

On the opposite end of the appearance spectrum are the rural areas of the country. Blue-jeans, overalls, and average clothes are the order of the day for many people living and working in rural areas. Here, people dressed elegantly are the exception rather than the rule. Rural people sometimes refer to nice clothes as "Sunday Go-A-Meeting" clothes, since they are primarily worn to church. Makeup is typically very basic and grooming standards largely non-existent. Cosmetic problems with teeth, skin, and other minor appearance related matters go mostly unchecked. Why? One reason relates directly to the types of industries centered around rural America. These industries typically include:

1) FARMING
2) LUMBER MILLING
3) COAL MINING
4) ENVIRONMENTAL CONSERVATION
5) FORESTRY
6) HIGHWAY REPAIR AND CONSTRUCTION
7) TOURIST ACTIVITIES SUCH AS HIKING, NATURE WATCHING, CANOE TRIPS, MOUNTAIN CLIMBING
8) GUIDING HUNTING OR FISHING PARTIES
9) SMALL, RETAIL BUSINESSES TO SUPPORT THE ABOVE INDUSTRIES

What is the common denominator to the above industries? They all tend to be labor and time-intensive. As you recall from Chapter 3, industries which tend to be labor intensive tend to ignore the appearance factor in job performance. In performing many of the above jobs, a person's appearance is actually negatively impacted. Many of these jobs require physical strength versus interpersonal (influencing) skills. They require a person to intermingle with the natural elements (mining, farming, forestry, etc.) in performance of the job. Since these jobs are also time-intensive, they allow little, if any, extra time for appearance-enhancing activities.

Appearance Rule #33

Areas whose economy relies on labor intensive and outdoor oriented industries TEND TO minimize the importance of a person's appearance (converse of Rule #31)

Proofs for Appearance Rule #33:

1. Would you expect farmers, construction workers, lumber jacks, and coal miners to maintain higher appearance standards than sales people, or even convenience store workers?

2. What types of words would describe an area whose economy is tied to factory production or warehouse operations? Would you expect workers to be dressed in expensive suits or work clothes?

3. Picture a coal miner or farmer coming home after work. What do you envision. Someone who appears clean as a whistle and nicely dressed or one who appears quite the opposite? If everyone in a given area (say a farming community) look

like you imagine at the end of a day, is there much incentive for them to change or look different (at days end)?

A second reason that rural areas are less sensitive to a person's appearance has to do with their relative isolation from media influence(s). Many areas have no daily newspaper delivery, printed media are usually in the form of mail order catalogs, television is watched infrequently or not at all (this may actually be a blessing!), radio is of local flavor and events, and most news centers around local happenings (church activities, personal injuries/illness, kid's mischief, etc.). People are isolated from the media (magazine, TV, Radio, etc.) ads, the makeup ads, the glamorous models, the appearance influence so prevalent in metropolitan areas. Advertising for makeup, skin care products, fancy suits, fancy dresses, and the like are infrequently seen. When these advertisements are seen, however, there is little identifiable need for the ad products due to the life-style and work-related activities which do not require these items. In general, the more isolated an area is from the media, the lower the appearance standard will be.

Appearance Rule #34

Areas relatively isolated to media influences (TV, radio, magazines, newspapers, etc.) OFTEN MAINTAIN lower appearance standards than do areas designated as "media mecca."

Proof for Appearance Rule #34

1. Ask yourself, "Do I truly believe that the media has no influence over our decision(s) to buy makeup, fancy clothes, etc.?" What about professional athletes telling which sneakers to wear, models telling us what perfume to use, etc.? Do you really think this has no effect on us as a society? I think you'll agree that the media does influence our lives (more than most of us care to admit).

Real Life Example of Rule #34

Take, for example, this story of a little town where I spent my summers and winters away from my boyhood home in metropolitan Philadelphia. This central Pennsylvania town of approximately 75 people is called Livonia. My father used to pick me up at school on Fridays in downtown Philadelphia and travel about 4 hours to this lodge in the middle of the Pennsylvania wilderness. Located midway between Lewisburg and State College, Pennsylvania on Route 192, Livonia was a "world" away from the metropolis of Philadelphia.

As we drove, the rock and roll music of the city gradually gave way to the "twang" of country music or music not played in the city for many years. Radio news broadcasts changed from stories of murder, political scandals, and huge traffic problems to reports of a car having gone off the road the previous night, cows on the loose, or happenings at the county fair. Traffic went from "stop and go" to us being practically the only ones on the road. Giant, impersonal supermarkets soon transformed into small country stores with "real" people behind the counters acting as if you had known them all your life. Conversation along the way went from fast-paced and curt to slow and polite language similar to a southern drawl (the accents of many people in Central Pennsylvania could easily be mistaken for those in Kentucky, Louisiana, and Tennessee).

Livonia was relatively isolated from media influences. There was one TV station available, one local AM radio station, and no local newspaper. There were no stores to buy magazines, papers, or cosmetics in town. The nearest "local" store, some 8 miles away, offered only limited access to papers, magazines, cosmetics and the like. There seemed a general lack of demand for these items as well.

Many town people worked in the rural occupations listed previously. These people were the plainest, yet nicest, people I have ever met. The most commonly worn clothes were typically faded, worn blue jeans along with flannel or work style shirts. I think in the seven or so years that I visited Livonia, I saw makeup on a woman maybe twice. Grooming was mostly confined to combing one's hair, unless a hat was worn to conceal "hat hair." Hat hair was the shape and style of a person's hair after a night of sleeping. Many of the townspeople's weekend hobbies and activities of the townspeople were those which required little appearance enhancement. These included:

A) Fishing
B) Hunting
C) Volleyball
D) Sewing
E) Canning
F) Gardening
G) Gathering or Splitting Wood
H) Picnicking
I) Camping
J) Going to the Centre county, Rebersburg town, or Pennsylvania state fair(s)
K) Mowing the lawn
L) Burning trash
M) Sighting in rifles
N) Scouting for deer/bear/turkey
O) Hanging out in local Bars (which resembled rustic lodges)
P) Going to the general store for groceries

All of the above activities require little or no appearance enhancement. Many are very similar to the occupations—time and labor intensive, and where participating in these activities may actually detract from one's appearance.

Immediately upon my arrival in Livonia, I changed from what was considered casual clothes for the Philadelphia school system in fear of being ridiculed as a "fancy city slicker." Yet somehow I found this place to be one of the most relaxing places in the world, perhaps due to its relative ignorance of appearance. Once past my perceived clothes barrier, people accepted me for what I was. Unlike the city, where I was subject to constant ridicule due to my weight, the people of Livonia made me feel comfortable and there was never even the slightest bit of appearance discrimination toward me or the other visitors to our lodge. Livonia was really a breath of fresh air for me since this was the first place I had been where I felt truly relaxed and unconcerned about possible personal ridicule. There existed a sort of unwritten code of acceptance whereby "flashy" people or the appearance-conscious were not to be trusted. These people were just good, "down home" folks unafraid of, or unconcerned with, appearances. They treated people for what they were, not what for the outward appearance they portrayed.

2. INDUSTRIAL AREAS WITHIN A METROPOLITAN AREA

Some metropolitan areas are so large they literally contain cities within cities. A metropolitan area is likely to contain areas ranging from very wealthy people to areas where people live on limited means. Areas that I've encountered which are typically insensitive to appearance are heavy industrial areas within a metropolitan area. Whether the area be a port, rail yard, heavy industry, warehouse, chemical, refinery, etc., it's likely that the area residents are mostly insensitive to a person's appearance.

Visit a local tavern in one of these areas and you'll find most patrons dressed in work clothes, wearing hats, and appearing somewhat grimy (particularly if they're coming from work). Similar to rural areas, metropolitan industrial areas concentrate on activities that are physically labor-intensive and jobs which detract from a person's appearance. People who are dressed and groomed well in these areas are much rarer than those dressed casually or in work clothes. People in these areas are mostly insensitive to a person's appearance. Average appearance and average clothes are the order of the day.

It has even been the case at times, that well dressed people or those who look "too nice" are actually shunned by the more average persons who are the norm. Being deemed "above" everyone else, overly attractive people don't fit the more of otherwise casual neighborhoods.

3. OTHER REGIONAL AREAS WHERE APPEARANCE IS UNIMPORTANT

a. FISHING FLEET VILLAGES

Many towns, where a large proportion of the economy relies on fishing, Crabbing, Clamming or other sea-harvesting ventures, tend to be less sensitive to a person's appearance. The townspeople worry more about the size of the days catch rather than their appearance which is irrelevant to the task at hand. Many fishermen and their support persons get up long before most city people even think of getting out of bed. Their appearance is not important to their livelihood and can be ignored, if so chosen.

b. CASUAL RESORT TOWNS

Many resort towns are very casual and tend to ignore a person's appearance. Since these towns foster casual environments, people vacationing there tend to dress and appear casual. Towns that come to mind are Wildwood, New Jersey, Lancaster County, Pennsylvania, Nags Head, North Carolina. I imagine you can add to the list from your experience.

c. NATIONAL OR STATE PARK AREAS

Can you imagine worrying about your appearance while camping, hiking, or mountain climbing? Why would anyone worry about appearance enhancement in such an environment unless they were going into town for dinner. Many people encountered at parks are as casual and relaxed looking as they can be. You wouldn't know a CEO from a farmer in this environment. That's exactly why people go to these parks, to unwind, relax, and be themselves!

d. MIDDLE CLASS CITY & TOWN NEIGHBORHOODS

Service related sections of the city which rely on semi or unskilled labor tend to ignore appearance. Service industries include fast food restaurants, retail stores, neighborhood diners, bars/taverns, lumber stores, package delivery, etc.. Accomplishment of jobs in these industries requires little or no appearance enhancement. Appearance tends to be average in neighborhoods relying on these occupations and there is no pressure for appearance improvement. Average is normal in such an environment.

II. HOW A PERSON'S AGE & EXPERIENCE AFFECTS THEIR TREATMENT OF YOUR APPEARANCE

They say the older a person gets, the wiser they get. This certainly holds true regarding a person's appearance. Many younger people are attracted to those who appear beautiful and very attractive. They feel compelled to befriend persons of optimum appearance and typically have little experience dealing with either average or unattractive persons. This lack of experience causes younger people to seek out those most pleasurable to view. They (younger people) tend to disproportionately utilize appearance as the primary discriminator of a person's worth, desirability and personality traits (warmth, honesty, temperament, etc.).

As people mature, their attention tends to shift away from appearance to factors such as honesty, openness, sense of humor, personal integrity, etc.. People are judged more on their merit rather than the assumption that attractive persons are inherently desirable and unattractive persons are inherently undesirable. The more experience a person has, the wider range of people they are likely to meet. These people include:

1. Attractive, self-centered "Jerks"
2. Attractive "manipulators"
3. Attractive and arrogant
4. Attractive and withdrawn
5. Attractive and mentally unstable
6. Attractive and lazy
7. Unattractive and intellectually gifted
8. Unattractive and highly educated
9. Unattractive and extremely personable
10. Unattractive and extremely caring/generous
11. Unattractive and motivated, ambitious, enthusiastic

Older persons, based on their expanded experience with people, do not assume that an attractive person is inherently wiser, more motivated, more honest, more intelligent, more hygienic, etc., than an unattractive person. They become more wary (of people) and tend to judge people on their own accord, rather than automatically stereotyping and making unwarranted assumptions.

Appearance Rule #35

The older one becomes, the LESS LIKELY they are to make assumptions about a person based solely on appearance provided they had exposure to persons who disprove the paradigm that "attractive persons are inherently valuable and unattractive persons are inherently of little value", and they understand the lesson provided by the contradiction afforded by this paradigm.

Proofs for Appearance Rule #35:

1) Ever met someone who is very attractive and who is also self-centered, arrogant, in love with themselves, or downright mean? If you have, has this not changed (or confirmed) your perception that attractive people are not necessarily, automatically "nice" people?

2) Ever meet an unattractive person who was extremely gifted mentally, very interesting or stimulating to talk with, or extremely nice generous, truly a genuine person? If you have, has this not changed your perception that unattractive people are not necessarily and automatically people who are bad and therefore should be avoided?

3) As you've gotten older, and maybe something less than perfect in your own appearance, have you not become less sensitive and more accepting of other people's appearances?

Remember the dating scene covered in Chapter 2. Younger people tend to over-emphasize their dating partner's appearance. They want it all and try to find someone who maximizes all characteristics such as attractiveness, honesty, integrity, mental capacity, etc.. Research has proven that, as people get older, they place much less emphasis on appearance than on factors such as goal compatibility, personality compatibility and factors relating more to the inner person rather than outer person. This shift away from appearance is more pronounced and typically occurs faster for women but happens to both sexes. As people get older they learn that they can't live long with an attractive person who is incompatible in other ways.

A person's experience (and upbringing) also plays heavily into the way they treat others based on appearance. If an individual was brought up believing that attractive people are inherently good or that unattractive people are not good (or that persons from certain races or ethnic origins are bad), then this early education will require many contradictory experiences to change that person's view.

The older a person is, the higher the probability that they would have experienced at least one such contradictory encounter!

The concept of older persons assuming less of others they meet depends on the level of their intelligence and education. If a person develops educationally and intellectually, people will be more apt to make few assumptions and judge people on their individual merits. If a person does not develop educationally and intellectually, then stereotyping and basic assumptions will continue well into the golden years. Many uneducated persons are very prejudicial well into their very late twilight years. The affect of intellectual ability and education is covered in detail next.

III. HOW A PERSON'S EDUCATION & INTELLIGENCE AFFECTS THEIR TREATMENT OF YOUR APPEARANCE

People like and tend to value people who are much like themselves. Likewise, people who are educated and intelligent value others who are also educated and intelligent, and those who can carry on intelligent, challenging, and enlightening conversations. Educated and intelligent people tend to be more analytical, more introspective, and tend to mentally process and judge each event, person, and situation on their own merits. These people, therefore, are less likely to discriminate and stereotype based on a person's appearance.

Let's look at some examples. R & D "think tanks" and Engineering labs are filled with highly intellectual, highly educated people who are typically not noted for maintaining (or being concerned with maintaining) a very attractive appearance. More typically, these work environments are likely to be casual and informal in nature, and designed to encourage intellectual or creative contributions versus maintaining one's appearance. Some people from these environments have been called derogatory names such as "nerds", "geeks", "weirdoes", "book worms", etc., due to their uniquely relaxed, different style (appearance). These people typically wear, act, and do things out of the ordinary which results in the (unwarranted) ridicule. These things include:

1. Wearing "pocket protectors."
2. Wearing dark or horned-rimmed eye glasses.
3. Wearing out-dated clothes.
4. Wearing "high water" pants (or "flood" pants).
5. Wearing calculators on their belts.
6. Attending Sci-Fi conventions and meetings.
7. Admit to being Star-Trekkies.
8. Display a "weird" sense of humor.
9. Appear socially awkward.
10. Display atypical laughs.
11. Interact (socialize) with their computer terminals far more than with people.
12. Talking almost exclusively about equations, algorithms, and technology.
13. Bragging about the speed of their computer processor chip.
14. Talking excessively about the Internet or Internet interactions.

While these people are indeed somewhat rare in the intellectual community, they tend to earn the stereotype for any associated with intellectual endeavors. People not from these intellectual environments tend to misunderstand the motivation of maintaining a substandard appearance (i.e. one unlike their own). People outside these environments tend to overlook the fact that intellectuals excel for reasons other than their appearance. In addition, people from outside intellectual environments tend to overlook that what is "good" for them in terms of achievement (appearance), is not necessarily key to achievement for intellectuals.

As an Engineer by trade, I have had women I dated tell me that I "don't look like an Engineer" (kind of a left handed compliment, I guess). When queried about what they mean, they've typically responded with "You don't look like the typical Engineer—you know, kind of nerdy" or, "You seem down to earth, not like some Engineers I have met", or (better yet) "I would have never guessed you were an Engineer, you are actually very romantic!" They all seemed quick to make judgments and stereotype me based on previous encounters. They also tended to place little value on persons who appeared less than "standard." These stereotypes were all formed by people who were not intellectually-oriented. These were people who made their living in occupations which relied heavily on appearance (sales clerks, marketing representatives, receptionists, models, etc.). Unlike intellectuals, these people did not process information or judge each situation on its own merit. They were limited by their mental ability and lack of comparable experience to that of an intellectual. It is rather ironic, that even though I appeared similar to these non-intellectuals and was compatible in appearance, I decided to not further pursue dating relationships with these women, since they were basically mentally unstimulating.

Who are some intellectual people we can point to in history? What about Albert Einstein, Stephen Hawking, Indira Ghandi, Robert Oppenheimer and other Physicists on the Manhattan (A-Bomb) project? These people are all considered to be among the most intellectual people of our times. They have made significant contributions to our society. Their intellectual ability is legendary. None of them were known for their appearance, nor did it affect their contributions. Einstein for example, maintained a unique hair style that was totally uncharacteristic of the times (1940's). The success paradigms for these famous people were associated with intellectual ability not appearance. They understood the importance of appearance but valued intellectual ability more! Their pattern(s) for success revolved around their principle asset—mental ability.

For others, the paradigm for success might center around appearance, influence abilities, friendliness, helpfulness, etc.. The following table describes some occupation paradigms:

Occupation	*Paradigm(s) for Success*
Scientist	Intellectual Ability
Scientist's Manager	Intellect & Influence
Sales	Appearance and Influence
Receptionist	Appearance, Friendliness, Organization Skills
Television News Anchor	Appearance, Voice, and Presentation Skills

APPEARANCE IS EVERYTHING

Occupation	_Paradigm(s) for Success_
Red Cross Worker	Friendliness/Helpfulness
Clothing Model	Appearance
Construction Worker	Physical Strength & Manual Dexterity
Farmer	Hard Work & Perseverance
University Professor	Knowledge & Presentation

We can see from the above chart that, depending on the paradigm for success, different traits will be valued for the occupation in question. Those whose occupation and success rely on appearance will be very conscious of their own and others' appearance. Conversely, those whose occupation and success rely on intellectual ability will tend to emphasize intellect, knowledge, and organization more than appearance.

Appearance Rule #36

People whose success relies primarily on appearance WILL TEND to value and be sensitive their own appearance as they WILL TEND to value people with similar appearance. In this instance, the perception that "what brings success to me is good, therefore what is good for me (attractive appearance) must then be good for others." The same perception holds true for intelligence, knowledge, physical strength, etc. (this is one reason we tend to gravitate towards those with similar "values").

Proofs for Appearance Rule #36:

1. You've made your living as a model and become wealthy as a result of your attractive appearance. You have worked very hard watching your weight, working out, eating healthy, etc., to achieve and maintain your success. You are constantly surrounded by other successful people who have worked just as hard and also look very attractive. How sympathetic would you be to someone who is not selected for a modeling job because they are slightly overweight and obviously haven't worked as hard as you have? Aren't their values "out of whack" with yours? "If they valued their appearance, they would have worked harder!"

2. You made it to the top of a marketing firm due to your impeccable appearance and customer presentation skills. You were told many times that you "swung the deal" due to your attention to detail and sharp presence in front of the customer. A new person is hired and travels to a prospective customer's site with you. Their appearance is less than stunning (pants hemmed too high, hair not combed, shirttail sticking out, etc.). What would you think? Would you "value their differences" or think "this person needs to shape up?" I personally would be more than a little annoyed!

3. You've made your living working as an auto mechanic. You take pride in studying the latest repair techniques, trends, model differences, etc.. You truly feel knowledgeable and professional. Along comes somebody "putting in their time", who

could care less about learning anything except that which is needed "to get by." As a result, they take much longer (than you) to effect repairs and make many more mistakes, and could "care less." Would you value someone who maintains a (value) system so different from your own? I seriously doubt it! Would you be more inclined to befriend this person or someone more like yourself?

Of the ten smartest people I've met, nine had a notable idiosyncratic appearance tendency. These people were consistently unattractive in terms of grooming, clothing, personal hygiene, or body shape. However, they were so creative and intelligent that their minds "became them." They existed largely in their minds, and tended to ignore their body and outward appearance. These people also tended to ignore, and be ignorant of, the appearance of others. They were more interested in knowing how smart you were or how nice you were rather than how you looked. These people were the least appearance discriminatory people that I've ever met. Appearance played little in their quest for success. Therefore, from their viewpoint, appearance had little importance in their judgment of others. I interviewed one extremely intelligent person for this book to determine their view on the situation. Here is what they said:

> "I look at each person individually and judge people by how they treat others and how much they have to contribute. I'm smart enough to know that there are those who are attractive, but who are worthless, and those who are unattractive but worth their weight in gold. I've never been too concerned with my appearance." (When asked why)...Because I've always been to busy studying, creating, doing other things related to my job to worry about my appearance—It hasn't seemed to hurt my chances for getting ahead in life."

This person is a Lead Scientist for a major computer company in the United States and is accomplished both from a monetary and an intellectual standpoint. This person maintains relatively poor hygiene, is very overweight, out of shape, and has never had a real date in his life. He's also high on my list of those least likely to discriminate based on appearance!

To summarize, people with superior intellectual ability or high levels of education generally do not discriminate based on appearance and are less sensitive towards the appearance of others because:

1. They are more capable of judging and mentally processing each person encountered. This enhanced mental processing reduces the chances for stereotyping, grouping, and making assumptions about people based on appearance.

2. Intellectuals and scholars tend to value others with intellectual ability. The value placed on intellect and knowledge comes, many times, at the expense of appearance.

3. Persons who contribute most to an intellectual or scholastic endeavor are likely to be from varied appearance categories. Appearance, therefore, is irrelevant to accomplishment in these realms.

4. Some of the most intellectual people in history were not very attractive at all. Some of the smartest people in the world are actually appearance-eccentric.

Chart 5 illustrates the relationship between education, intelligence, and appearance discrimination. It basically illustrates that, "The more educated and intelligent a person is, the less likely they will make assumptions about a person based on their appearance." This is particularly true if a person is older, wiser, and has had more experience with people of varied appearances.

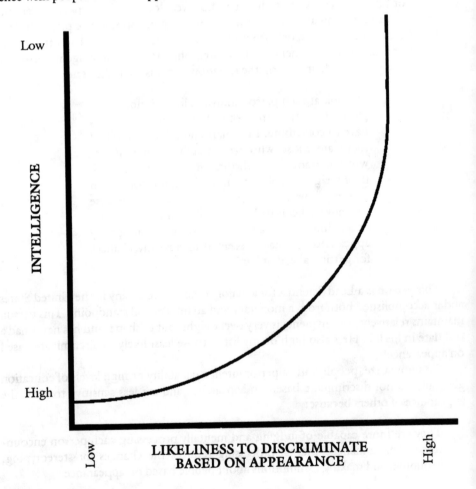

Relationship Between Intelligence & Appearance Discrimination
Chart 6

CHAPTER 5 SUMMARY

A. Metropolitan areas tend to have many layers of affluence and proportionally higher appearance standards.

B. The most affluent and attractive people tend to gravitate toward metropolitan areas.

C. Affluent non-metropolitan areas also uphold higher appearance standards.

D. Areas such as Hollywood, California, whose economies rely on appearance, are magnets to, and havens for, the attractive.

E. Affluent resort towns, affluent marine traffic areas, and areas whose culture encourages wealth and achievement, all maintain higher appearance standards.

F. Certain geographic areas of the United States hold appearance in higher regard than other regions.

G. Rural areas maintain a much lower appearance standard than metropolitan areas due to the type of industries prevalent.

H. Areas which rely on influence industries (sales, marketing, public relations, brokering, acting, television, modeling, etc.) tend to maintain higher appearance standards.

I. Areas which rely on physical labor-intensive industries tend to maintain a lower appearance standard.

J. The appearance standard is set lower in areas such as inner city industrial areas, state and national parks, middle income service areas within a city, and certain fishing villages.

K. As people get older and wiser, they tend to diminish the importance of appearance.

L. Older people have typically met a wider range of people ranging from Attractive jerks to Unattractive geniuses and tend to learn that attractive people should not be automatically assumed as valuable/desirable and unattractive people should not be automatically assumed not valuable/undesirable.

M. Older people tend to shift from stressing attractiveness in personal relationships to personality traits such as compatibility, honesty, integrity, etc..

N. Older persons must be wise enough to appreciate the lessons in letter L above.

O. Intellectuals tend to judge each person individually on their own merits, rather than making assumptions based on appearance alone.

P. Intellectuals tend to value the intellectual ability and knowledge of others, rather than appearance.

Q. Some intellectuals tend to overlook their own appearance since it is has played such a minimal role in their success as compared to intellect.

R. People tend to gravitate toward others who maintain similar paradigms and value systems for success (i.e. intellectuals to intellectuals, attractive to attractive, etc.)

S. People who have been successful via their attractive appearance tend not to understand those who do not maintain their appearance.

T. People who have been successful via their intellect tend not to relate to people who are appearance-driven.

CHAPTER
6

WHERE DOES IT ALL BEGIN?

As you read to this point, you may have asked yourself "does appearance discrimination only occur at the adult level, or is this something that starts much earlier?" If it does start early on, then what influences cause Appearance Discrimination to emerge?

Our research found appearance discrimination present in every stage throughout one's lifetime. However, the issues of Appearance Discrimination that relate to adults differ with children. For example, careers, dating, relationships, and marriage as opposed to discipline, treatment in school, and overall treatment/acceptance by adults.

The way children are treated by parents, teachers, coaches, peers, and adults in general contributes significantly to their inner development. As we found in Chapter 4, repeated praise and encouragement tend to support strong self-esteem and establish a high level of self-confidence. Conversely, repeated "put downs" for a variety of reasons, or even one specific thing (e.g. "you're fat" or "you're stupid"), may result in the recipient growing up believing this is so. Clearly the utterly destructive, low self-esteem begins to develop early on in life

Many studies have been conducted and books written about child development. Some such studies analyze the issue of children's appearance as it relates to their development. Several doctors and psychologists reported the following findings:

A. INFANTS

Many will agree that one of the greatest moments of pride and joy can be the birth of a new baby, particularly for the proud parents. The first questions after "is it a boy or a girl?" are typically, "ten fingers?, ten toes?, is the baby all right?, who does it look like?" Reactions such as these are common and accompanied by a sense of relief and happiness when the new parents find out that "everything is just fine." Another common (and natural) reaction is the immediate urge to show off the new baby and bask in the showers of praise about your new addition that soon follow from family, friends, and even total strangers.

A popular women's magazine, "Woman's World", features a column entitled, "Your Beautiful Baby", where readers are encouraged to send snapshots of their "beautiful" babies in the most "adorable" poses for inclusion in the magazine. Contributors (probably parents and grandparents) are asked to include a caption about the child along with the photo. A sampling of captions follows:

"My 11-month old grand-daughter found her breakfast cereal good to the last bite, but if you ask me, she's the real dish. I could just eat her up!"

"Our seven month old baby isn't just one of the bunch, he's the top banana in this family—and he knows it."

"My three-month old daughter was tickled pink to have her picture taken. She loved all the attention. And it's a good thing, because she's so cute, she's going to attract lots of it!"

This is certainly quite common, and almost expected, behavior. Proud parents and their families are always eager to show off and draw attention to their attractive children. While this has probably been going on since mothers have been having babies, and will likely continue on through time, is this not the beginning of children learning (albeit subconsciously) about appearance differences? Is this not how children learn that they differ from other (less attractive) children because they may be more attractive and thus attract more attention? Does this not point out some early signs of the attractive "haves" and unattractive "have-nots?"

What about the reaction to a child born with some sort of blemish or disfigurement? Is the reaction the same? A 1979 report talks about the reactions of parents whose children are born with some sort of physical disfigurement states that new parents typically showed less pride in their newborn child and were less willing to show off their offspring than other parents. You may say this is a natural reaction, "they're only trying to protect their baby from comments and ridicule." Still, the bottom line goes back to the whole issue of appearance. Everyone who has a child wants other people to react with "oh how cute!, he/she is adorable!, what a beautiful baby!" When these things cannot be said, parents tend to retreat and are less apt to "show off" their newborn. Thus, the appearance discrimination cycle begins!

We asked a group of new parents (of normal babies) to share some of the reactions they received from anxious admirers:

1. "How cute"
2. "Adorable"
3. "What a beautiful baby"
4. "How precious"
5. "He/she is so sweet"
6. "What a little angel"
7. "He/she is going to be a heart-breaker someday"

A person's sense of self begins to develop in our earliest days. Attractive "cute" children that become the center of attention among parents, grandparents, other family members, etc., receive numerous positive reinforcements which begin to form the way that child feels about him/herself. The more attention they receive, the more they are told how adorable or cute they are, the more they will begin to believe it, and form a positive self-image.

While more uncomfortable to think about or even discuss, parents of less attractive children report that polite smiles or total avoidance replace the praise lauded to other children.

What is this all about? Does it not emphasize the importance of appearance in its earliest form? A number of reports examine children's social development based on their appearance and how others react to them because of the way they look.

K. Dion conducted some interesting studies based on different theories whereby children are perceived and treated based on the way they look. One study was based on the theory that unattractive children are assumed to be more unpleasant and dishonest than attractive children.

Are these children truly more unpleasant because they lack the continuous praise and positive compliments received by more attractive children? Might they actually be somewhat dishonest because they are hungry for attention and therefore engage in more mischievous behavior to gain that attention? It certainly is a thought provoking suggestion and one that can be supported as we look at how attractive and unattractive children develop.

V. McCabe hypothesized that physically abused children had atypical cranial/facial proportions which, in turn, affected their treatment by adults. While this theory is rather controversial and no strong arguments support the idea, it is yet another example that suggests that children are treated differently based on the way they look.

Other research conducted by Stephan and Langlois in 1984 was based on their hypothesis that suggests adults expect facially unattractive infants to cause their parents problems. Their research was conducted by showing a group of college students photographs of infants aged 3 and 9 months. The students were asked first to rate the infants first on attractiveness and next on other factors—good baby, healthy, cheerful, attached to mother, responsive to other people, cute, active, persistent, smart, likable, and "causes parents problems."

All these determinations were based solely on photographs. The findings of this exercise confirmed to the hypothesis that the more attractive infants were the ones labelled "good baby", "cute", "healthy", "cheerful", "smart", "likeable", etc., while unattractive infants were assumed to be less pleasant and more likely to cause problems for their parents.

Does this exercise cause you to believe that from the earliest stages we are categorized based on our appearance and that other people's expectations of us or our assumed personality (by total strangers) is based on what we look like? This is just another example of how we are exposed to appearance discrimination throughout every phase of our lives.

The next pages discuss the question "at what age are children aware of appearance differences", and will also review studies that examine how children are disciplined, what expectations are placed on them in school, athletic performance, and their overall success in life based on the way they look.

B. AT WHAT AGE ARE CHILDREN AWARE OF APPEARANCE DIFFERENCES?

While there can be no question that we, as adults, make judgments about other people's appearance, it is not known for certain at what age children begin to differentiate between what is visually (more or less) attractive.

Back in the mid 1960's, a team of psychologists, Kagan, Henker, Hen-Tov, Levine and Lewis, studied the reaction of infants aged 4 and 8 months to a variety of three dimensional models of "faces."

The infants were shown four different faces—one was "normal looking" with 2 eyes, a nose, and a mouth; the other three faces were scrambled or distorted in some way. The psychologists showed each infant the photographs, then measured the length of time that the child studied each face. The end results showed that the infants repeatedly held a longer gaze at the "normal" face.

While this study does not concretely prove that the infants found one face more pleasing than the other, it does point out rather strong evidence that these infants could differentiate between various face formations, and perhaps the length of their gazes was a result of that which they found "more appealing."

How did these infants learn to differentiate between appearance? Is this something they learned? Or is this something biological that people are born with?

You may say, "so what, is this such a profound finding?" Probably not. However, the main reason for mentioning this exercise is to point out that appearance discrimination (or differentiation) is something that we experience and engage in from our earliest years.

C. DIFFERENTIAL TREATMENT BASED ON A CHILD'S APPEARANCE

There have also been studies conducted that look at how children are disciplined and whether or not appearance has anything to do with the frequency and type of discipline they receive. It has been suggested that less attractive children are disciplined more frequently and not expected to achieve at the same level in life as more attractive children.

A 1975 J. Rich study looked at how blame may be placed on a child for a wrong doing based on people's unconscious reactions to different children's appearance. In his study, Rich used a group of female schoolteachers as his subjects. He gave each of them written details of an incident in school where a child was tripped by a classmate and fell down a flight of stairs. The teachers were asked to imagine the incident in their minds and to also imagine the other children standing at the top of the stairs, one of whom tripped the child. They were told that all of the children denied pushing the other child, but several children were "glancing" toward one particular child who had a slight grin.

The next part of the exercise involved showing the teachers supposed photographs of the grinning child. Some photographs were attractive, some unattractive. The teachers were then asked to react to the photographs by:

1) Stating how strongly they felt that the child in the photograph had committed the misbehavior.

2) Rate the child on seven personality scales.

3) Commenting on the extent to which the child should be punished and the severity of punishment, assuming that the child had committed the misbehavior.

The findings showed that unattractive boys received more blame and were recommended for stronger punishment than did attractive boys! The unattractive boys also received lower ratings on the seven personality scales.

Unfair you say? Think how often this happens in everyday life. How often are judgements placed against us, some of which are totally unjustified, simply because of our appearance? The above exercise simply points out that this happens throughout our lives, whether we are willing to admit it or not. One further disturbing outcome of the above exercise revolves around the lower personality ratings received by the unattractive children. These findings add proof to the suggestion that less attractive children (and later adults) are subjected to different levels of expectations (personality, intelligence, ability to achieve) than their more attractive peers.

Another important finding is that appearance affects children's academic performance. Consider the following passage from the book, The Social Psychology of Facial Appearance:

"Landy and Signall (1974) asked male college students to evaluate an essay (on the effects of television on society) supposedly written by a female college student. The students were told that the essays were to be entered in a contest run by a television station and because of this some background about the author of each essay was provided. By means of a photograph attached to each essay some of the evaluators were led to believe that the essay writer was physically attractive and others that she was unattractive. In addition, one half of the students read an essay that was well written, grammatically correct, organized and clear in its presentation of ideas, whereas the other subjects read the essay that was poorly written, disorganized, and simplistic. Subjects' evaluations of the essay were significantly affected by attractiveness for the poor essay but not for the good essay. Landy and Signall made an interesting speculation concerning this statistical interaction effect when they put forward the idea that if a person's work is competent then personal appearance may be less likely to influence evaluations of that work than when the quality of work is poor. They suggested that if you are ugly you are not discriminated against a great deal as long as

your performance is impressive. However, should
your performance be below par, attractiveness matters: you may be able to get away with inferior work
if you are beautiful."

D. APPEARANCE FACTORS WHICH INFLUENCE CHILDREN

As stated earlier, we are influenced by many factors throughout our lives. However, children may be considered more vulnerable "targets" of influence because of their
innocence and naivete. Parents and other significant adults in the lives of children can
influence their development tremendously. Children may have many role models
throughout their life. Depending on their particular appeal, some of these role models
will have more impact than others. Some will likely have a more positive influence than
others, but nonetheless, they all make some kind of an impression!

The following is a list of "influencers" on young children and adolescents that introduce them to the materialistic, consumer-oriented, electronically-driven, sound
bite-oriented, and highly stimulated world around them:

1. Parents/Significant Adult
2. Peer Pressure
3. Television
4. Other * Magazines * Toys * Clothes

1. Parent/Significant Adult

Parents are, by far, in most children's lives, the most influential person(s) in their
development. In non-traditional families, the significant adult—grandparent, brother,
sister, aunt, uncle, caregiver, etc., are all very influential in the development of the
child(ren) for which they are responsible. While these influences may not always be
good (or positive), they all have a major impact on a child's development!

Our parents introduce us to the world around us and are our initial teachers. They
instill values, set rules, and give us principles to live by that are largely based on their
own values, beliefs, and experiences. As adults, we can look back and remember things
our own parents used to say to us, things they did, beliefs they held, and see traces (of
our parents) in ourselves.

It stands to reason that many opinions we have formed about what is attractive and
what is not attractive were learned from our parents. It also stands to reason that the
more appearance conscience your parents were when you were growing up, the more
likely that you are conscience about your appearance.

Appearance Rule #37

*The more we learn as children to be aware of our own appearance, the more aware
and sensitive we will tend to be about other people's appearance as adults.*

If we grew up with parents who were very conscious of their own appearance,
chances are that they were also very conscience about their children's (our) appear-

ance. Appearance in this context refers not only to physical characteristics, but more inclusively and more importantly, to the way we take care of ourselves—grooming, clothing, healthy life-styles, etc..

We asked a group of people to think back to some of the things their parents used to say to them when they were growing up that were appearance related. The things they remembered and shared with us were not surprising. Here's a sampling:

"Don't eat too much junk food—you'll get fat"
"Eat good foods—you'll grow up to be big and strong"
"What are you wearing? Don't go out of this house looking like that!"
"What have you done with your hair?"
"Keep your hands out of your pockets and stand up straight!"

As the group reminisced and shared their thoughts, they commented that, even though they were all from different families, there were common themes surrounding what their parents/caregivers had said in order to teach them good habits.

Our small, control group was made up of 10 people, ages 28 to 40, all Category 3's and low 2's. They are well groomed and maintain healthy life-styles. While none will admit to being "obsessed", they will admit that their appearance is very important (to them).

When asked what they think contributed to this they readily admit that it has a lot to do with the way they were raised and the influences that were around them. One interesting fact, however, was that some stated that they had adopted healthier life-styles even though their parents did not!

Several group members talked about how their parents always encouraged, and even demanded, that their children eat right and take care of themselves, but did not always follow their own advice. While the majority of the group said that their parents were both appearance and health conscious, others were committed to a healthier life-style because they had seen the consequences of not caring and not taking care of one-self!

Several people had parents who may have been thin and healthy in their earlier years, but as they aged, paid less attention to what they ate, whether or not they exercised, and paid much less attention to their overall appearance. As a result of their lackadaisical behaviors, some of these parents are now overweight, out of shape, and suffer continuously with ill health. While this is certainly not a good situation (for their parents), these children learned by example. They realized that many of their parents' health problems could have been eliminated, or at least minimized, if they had just taken better care of themselves. These children realize that bad habits such as "letting yourself go" and generally not caring about yourself can lead to later problems in life and, they have learned from their parents' mistakes!

The later part of Rule #37 mentions sensitivity to others' appearance. Certainly, if we grow up in an environment where appearance is important, and we learn to become conscientious about our own appearance, more than likely we will also learn to take notice of other people's appearance. Many of our parents' perceptions of what is (and is not) attractive become our perceptions of the same. Comments made about other people and the way parents treat others is often times mimicked and repeated by (their) children.

Parents who point out other peoples' flaws, are critical of others appearance, and tendency to tease other people, will have children who do the same. Does any of this sound familiar?

1) "Look how fat that person is!"
2) "He/She is so homely"
3) "Look at that person's hair"
4) "I can't believe the outfit that person has on!"

What kind of influences were part of your life when you were growing up?

As children, we are not usually mature enough to realize that this sort of behavior is unkind and inappropriate, especially when we hear these things coming from our own Mom and Dad! It is usually only after we have matured somewhat that we may make a conscious effort to change our behavior towards other people (regardless of our parents).

2. Peer Pressure

Peer pressure and a child's appearance have a significant affect on their development and sense of self. Peer pressure amongst children, and later teenagers, can be very constructive. At other times it can be so destructive that children and young adults will remember throughout their lifetime(s) the names they were called by other children and the situations that caused them to feel degraded and demeaned by those around them!

Young children are exposed to peer pressure at different ages, depending upon how early they are exposed to other children and adults outside their own home. In today's society, many children are in Day Care Centers or with baby-sitters outside the home, people who may be "watching" several other children simultaneously (a rather sensitive topic today). Being in an environment with other children can be very positive in the development of socialization skills through interactions with these other children and/or adults. These situations also expose children (at earlier ages) to name calling and teasing. In situations where a child is more sheltered and has not had the same opportunities to interact with other children at an early age, it can be devastating to suddenly be (put) in a situation where they are teased and called names!

The following is a real life example of a child who was not exposed to other children on a regular basis and how she was not prepared for the teasing and name calling that is (unfortunately) a part of entering Kindergarten.

Suzie was the first child of a young professional couple who both worked outside the home, but on different schedules. Her Dad worked a typical 9-5 day, but Mom worked 3-11PM. Suzie would be home until Mom went to work and then spend the remainder of the afternoon with her grandparents who lived just a block away. She would later spend the evening hours with her Dad after he got out of work.

While this was really a good arrangement in many ways—it was very convenient,

Suzie was able to spend maximum time with her parents and grandparents, she had basically very little interaction with other children her own age.

Suzie was a friendly, polite, well-behaved child who truly enjoyed contact with other children. She was excited about beginning Kindergarten and knew that would be an opportunity to meet other youngsters. She made an easy transition into school and looked forward to going each day. She had met classmates and talked about the other children frequently.

One day Suzie came home from school quite upset. After some probing, her parents learned that one of her classmates, a boy, was teasing her and told her she was "fat." Children are going to be teased by other children—it is part of going to school and growing up, but, given that Suzie had come from a more sheltered environment, she was totally taken aback and very disturbed when she became the object of this teasing.

Her Mom later noticed that (suddenly) "fat" or "fatty" became a regular part of Suzie's vocabulary. When she was angry with something or upset she would call the object, or person, fat—"he's fat, she's fat"—obviously associating with the anger she felt when called the same name.

As children get older, peer pressure continues, and almost invariably, worsens. I think back to my years in Junior High School and High School and am thankful that those years are behind me. I vividly remember worrying about "fitting in"—"did he or she like me?", "what did they think of me?" Many adolescents and teens are so "hung up" on "fitting in" and "being accepted" (by the crowd), that they are not their own person because if the fear that they may be rejected if they voice a different opinion or present a different appearance!

A clear example of just such peer pressure became very clear as I flipped through a recent edition of "TEEN" magazine. Below is a list of some of the articles/columns I came across:

"The how-to-look-perfect prom guide"
"How girls look—what he loves, what he hates"
"Are you a leader of the pack or someone who's more comfortable being part of the crowd? Take our quiz and find out your leadership quotient!"
"Why would you date someone really different than yourself? (taller, heavier, different religion, race, etc.)"
"Secrets of girls who get dates—five ways to win him over"
"Tips for *perfect* prom pictures"

This is not meant as a criticism of a popular magazine, but rather a statement about how important it is to look good, wear the latest clothing, sport the latest hair style, act the right way, in order to be accepted as part of the crowd.

The list of magazines and advertisements is virtually endless but the focus stays the same.

Another dimension of peer pressure has to do with the "cliques." Think back to when you were in junior high, or high, school—do any of the following (groups) sound familiar to you?

APPEARANCE IS EVERYTHING

1) Jocks
2) Cheerleaders
3) Nerds (usually the smarter, but less social, group)
4) Cool kids
5) Dorks (not accepted by cool kids and typcially not academically inclined)
6) Druggies/Losers

While the names may have changed through the years, the meanings and divisions of these groups have common themes. There are always those that identify with one or more group or clique. There are also those, while less common, who fit into no social group comfortably.

Peer pressure reaches its peak during the high school years and then seems to lessen once students graduate and go off to college. While the high school peer influences are still present, the act of "breaking away" from (the daily contact of) the high school group, and going off to college or work, substantially lessens their influence. Once the break has been made, these young adults are apt to feel free to become their own person and less concerned with what others think!

The practice of wearing uniforms in private schools has everything to do with peer pressure. By mandating that all young men and women have a "uniform look", the pressure and competition often associated with clothing (i.e. what am I going to wear tomorrow?) is eliminated. There are, of course, other reasons why uniforms are standard in some schools, but the de-emphasizing of appearance tries to create an atmosphere where there are less divisions and students can concentrate more on studies and more serious (non-appearance related) endeavors.

3. Television

Television is probably the strongest outside influence on children today. Many children spend hours each day in front of the television, watching a wide spectrum of shows and commercials. These shows introduce young viewers to "what's in", "what's cool", who the current "heroes" are, and various "issues of concern" to their particular age group. Television can easily set the norm in an appearance-driven society (such as ours). Through television, young minds see images of attractive young actors and actresses sporting the latest clothes and hair styles, involved in the latest activities, talking the "in" slang or lingo. Through these examples, young children naturally draw their own conclusions about appearance, about what is acceptable!

Commercials, as part of television, are exceptionally strong (appearance) influences—introducing new products and brand names. Some of the following items immediately come to mind:

1) Sneakers
2) Jeans
3) Logos on Sweatshirts
4) Athletic Equipment

Television producers and advertising executives know all too well the power of this medium and the potential impact of a visual image. They cleverly schedule commercials according to who is likely to be viewing at a particular time. Specific commercials are scheduled for Saturday morning when the TV is filled with cartoons and children's shows, Monday through Friday between 3:00 and 6:00PM—right after school and before dinner. If you have the opportunity, tune in your TV for even one half hour during these times to see some of the influences we are talking about.

In just a half hour, you will probably see no less than 12 commercials for products ranging from the latest baby dolls and "Barbies", to Action Hero toys, breakfast cereals, fruit/soft drinks, candies, bicycles, and clothing geared to a young, impressionable, materialistic generation, a generation just beginning to get an idea of the appearance-driven world awaiting them!

We live in a highly visual society and younger people are easily drawn to the "glitz" and fast paced messages associated with commercials and music television. The current younger generation is frequently criticized for reading little or not at all, having poor SAT Verbal scores and atrocious writing skills because they spend more time in front of the TV than in reading a good book!

Advertisers and television producers are very aware of this and do whatever they can to appeal to this group at their level.

E. HOW YOU CAN MAKE A DIFFERENCE IN YOUR CHILD'S DEVELOPMENT

Regardless of outside influences, parents and adults can still make the biggest single contribution toward developing a child's positive self-image.

1. IGNORE THE INSULTS—TEACH CHILDREN TO BELIEVE IN THEMSELVES!

When we discussed peer pressure, we talked about how children are teased and called names, unfortunately a common part of growing up. The variable within this issue of name calling and being the recipient of degrading comments, is how we react to them. Certainly no one enjoys being ridiculed, teased, or called names. If children learn to ignore such comments and not "take them to heart", they will be much more adept in dealing with negative comments and criticism later on.

Remember the old saying, "sticks and stones may break my bones but names will never hurt me?" I heard it over and over again as I was growing up. My parents would recite this phrase to me whenever I was upset about being teased or ridiculed. This was their way of explaining to me that name calling meant very little and we (I) should learn to ignore it.

Parents should teach their children to believe in themselves, believe in their self-directed goals, believe they are worthy of (justifiable) praise, and resist the mean-spirited comments of others. Children can be very cruel to one another, particularly when it comes to name calling and teasing. When a child has low self-esteem and finds themselves the object of (another's) ridicule, it can be devastating, and could leave a deep mental wound that may last a long time.

APPEARANCE IS EVERYTHING

When children are raised in an environment that teaches them to believe in their own self-worth, they are much better equipped to deal with some of the adversity that they'll face throughout their life. They will also be better equipped to deal positively with other people, form friendships, and have lasting relationships.

Children should be encouraged to feel good about their physical appearance and not feel like less of a person because of (perceived) negative physical characteristics. Here are some examples of physical characteristics which tend to make children feel awkward and possibly the source of ridicule:

* Having freckles
* Wearing glasses
* Wearing braces
* Being too thin
* Being too fat
* Being too short
* Being too tall/gawky
* Having acne
* Entering puberty earlier/later than peers

On the other hand, it can be argued that too much praise and ego building in the early years can lead to an over-inflated ego which can be almost as harmful as low self-esteem. In some situations, parents and adults can go overboard in building up their child's ego.

Children that are continuously praised and told how pretty, how handsome, how smart they are, etc., can develop such a strong sense of self that they are later perceived as "cocky" or "self-centered." These children are also more likely to have difficulty getting along with others and developing solid, long-lasting friendships and relationships throughout their life!

Balance, therefore, is the key. By encouraging children to believe in themselves without being "cocky", and to disregard other people's (insensitive and inappropriate) comments, they will be more balanced individuals and better equipped emotionally to grow and learn throughout their life.

2. IMPROVEMENT IS OK, TO A POINT!

As children, we are taught to always strive to be the best we can—or even better. We also know that, while most of us all have things we'd like to improve about ourselves, the reality is that we all have limitations. This can be a hard lesson for children and, in some cases, an even harder lesson for parents

As a parent, it is important to be supportive and encouraging, but it is also important to recognize the level of ability and any limitations our children may possess. The following scenarios/situations come to mind as we think about instances where parental expectations may exceed the child's actual ability:

* Being the best Little League (or other sports) player
* Competing (and winning) Little Miss Pageants/Beauty Contests

* Unreasonable demands made on making Honor Roll or getting straight A's
* Having superior talent in Performing Arts-related activities—i.e. dancing, singing, acting, etc.

Every parent wants their child to do well and achieve success in life. However, parents must take care to not place so much pressure on a child to achieve that the child feels inadequate if those lofty expectations cannot be met. This type of pressure can be very destructive in a young person's life and lead to development of a negative self-worth.

Every little girl cannot be the next "Little Miss" and win beauty pageants. By the same token, all little boys are not so athletically inclined that they will be the star of the local little league or pee-wee football team.

Once again, balance is critical. Laziness and poor attitudes should not be tolerated, but recognizing when a child is truly trying their best, and praising those efforts, is very important! Parents should de-emphasize always "winning", always "being first", always being recognized as the "best" or "prettiest" and encourage their children to always "do their best." Remember another saying, "it's not whether you win or lose, but how you play the game."

3. THERE IS MORE TO LIFE THAN APPEARANCE

This entire book focuses on appearance and the affect appearance has on children and adults throughout their life. We mention appearance "quotients" and appearance "categories" and even take an appearance "test" to determine which category we fall into and which of our physical characteristics may (or may not) be considered attractive.

Appearance Rule #38

Just as we MUST RECOGNIZE (as adults) that we all have limitations and cannot be someone we are not, likewise WE MUST teach our children to recognize their strengths and value their differences

Proofs for Appearance Rule #38:

A clear message throughout this book has been that people have very different physical appearances. We all differ and all have various opportunities in life based on our physical appearance. Also, we all differ when it comes to personality, intelligence, personal motivation, etc. We must learn to recognize both our strengths and weaknesses, then learn to maximize our strengths. The earlier in life we learn this, the better off we will be!

Think about the following:

> Michael was a tall, slim child lacking physical strength. His dad, a former college football player, wanted nothing more than to have his son play (col-

legiate) football. Michael was pushed into playing junior league football and received much pressure from his dad to do well. He tried hard and gave football his best shot, but learned very quickly he was not cut out for the game, and was more interested in running track. His father was relentless and would not accept the fact that his son was not meant to play football. Rather than listening to his son and encouraging his interest in track and field, Michael's father made his son feel inadequate and a disappointment to his father because of his disinterest and physical limitations on the football field.

How many times have you known a parent to push their child into something simply because the parent wanted the child to be involved and the child had little or no interest? Many parents try to relive their own childhood through their children, and push them to excel and succeed in areas where the parent may have fallen short.

The following brief list describes some common situations where parents will push children into a situation without taking the child's actual abilities and interests into consideration:

* Participation in a specific sport
* Playing the piano or some other musical instrument
* Taking voice or acting lessons
* Trying out for cheerleading
* Pledging for a particular Fraternity or Sorority
* Enrolling in the same college Mom or Dad graduated from, or a very prestigious college

In order to develop and foster a child's positive self-image, parents must accept their children for what they are. This is not to suggest that necessary pushes are not important when needed, but that pushing too much in the wrong direction can be destructive.

CHAPTER 6 SUMMARY

A. Appearance Discrimination is present in every stage throughout a lifetime.
B. The way we are treated as children by parents, teachers, coaches, peers, and other adults, contributes significantly to our inner development.
C. New parents thrive on the praise and compliments given to their child.
D. Experiments have proven the hypothesis that certain perceptions are made, and treatment given, to children based on their appearance.
E. A study was conducted to prove or disprove the theory that unattractive children are assumed to be more unpleasant and more dishonest than attractive children.

F. It has been proven that infants as young as 4 months old can differentiate between various face formations and suggested that the length of their gaze is a result of what they find "more appealing."

G. It has been suggested that less attractive children are disciplined more frequently and are expected to achieve less in life than more attractive children.

H. Among the most significant appearance factors which influence children are: parents/significant adult, peers, and television.

I. The more we are educated as children to be aware of our own appearance, the more aware and sensitive we will be about other people's appearance.

J. Children should learn to ignore teasing and insults and believe in themselves.

K. Appearance improvement is good, obsession with appearance is not.

L. We must recognize our limits and not be someone we are not. Children should learn to maximize their strengths and value their differences.

CHAPTER
7

IMPROVING YOUR APPEARANCE QUOTIENT (AQ)

One of the best methods for avoiding appearance discrimination is eliminating the source of such treatment. By eliminating the source, we essentially "give them nothing to talk about" in regard to how we appear. It might seem like "giving in", but it is far easier to improve one's appearance than to educate people that appearance discrimination is wrong. In this instance, unlike race discrimination, there is much that one can do to eliminate the source of appearance discrimination. We will examine, in order of relative effectiveness, various methods for improving your appearance and why they are effective.

We'll look at the psychology of why people see you differently after implementing each method. Let's first look at the most effective form of appearance improvement—improving muscle tone.

A. IMPROVING MUSCLE TONE:

Improving muscle tone has many positive health effects. It embellishes your appearance while affecting all areas of your body. When working out we tend to stress the entire body while tightening muscles. We examined many persons who went from being completely out of shape to more muscular. One often overlooked benefit of muscle toning is the positive effect on facial features and facial muscles. The process of toning a person's body also has an effect on the shape, contour, and overall appearance of one's face, their most important appearance asset. We observed photographs of persons before they started exercising and after extended periods (months & years) of exercising. We were astonished that these people's faces actually tended to be more attractive. They went from having little or no facial contour (rounded, unnoticeable features, bland looking) to faces which were striking and more contoured. For example, the highly desirable feature of distinguished cheekbones were much more present after persons had gone through an exercise program. Facial features appeared less round, more sleek and discernible, and connoted physical strength. Research has proven this to be true. Lucker, a leading researcher, found:

"Faces judged to be unattractive to be "more convex" and have "greater soft tissue thickness in the lower third of the face."

Another researcher, Fitzgerald, found that infants rated as "cuter" had "short narrow features."

While we had no time to prove this correlation ourselves, we found that more Category 1's and 2's had practiced some form of regular exercise program then had lower Appearance Category persons. We compiled the following list which highlights the positive appearance effects of exercise:

1. Enhanced facial appearance via increased visibility and contouring of positive facial features (clear facial lines, discernible cheekbones, dimples, etc.).

2. Enhanced contouring of other desirable body areas (buttocks, bosom, legs, arms, etc.) leading to aroused sexual and attractive tendencies. Men especially are attracted to women with toned buttocks and trim legs. Women tend to be attracted to men with toned chests, arms, and upper torsos.

3. Seemingly more capable, lean/agile person, capable of accomplishing more.

4. A higher energy level and more positive presence (attitude) which makes you more attractive (desirable) to be around.

5. A confident attitude and projected appearance due to positive psychological aspects of exercising.

6. For more muscular males, other males may sometimes be intimidated and treat you with more respect. Also, insecure or very small females will tend to seek out these very muscular males for protection and insulation from their own insecurity or slight frame.

By exercising regularly, you have the potential to significantly raise your AQ an average of 1 level (i.e. 2—>1, 3—>2, 4—>3). Beyond the physical and psychological benefits of exercising, your enhanced appearance and the improved way people treat you should also be strong incentive!

The benefits of exercise are enormous. It is as if some sort of natural selection process takes place. By exercising we make ourselves more capable, healthier, and more energetic. Could some sort of facial signal take place which alerts others and potential mates that those who exercise are indeed healthier, more capable, and more likely of producing healthy offspring, etc.? In man's early (cave) days, those who were most physically capable mated with the most attractive/fertile females. Greater physical accomplishments (at that time) translated into more food, greater protection, higher respect and more resource allocations. Could an unconscious mechanism still be in place which allows us to recognize and be drawn towards those most physically capable via a facial feature signal mechanism? It would be intriguing to study this phenomenon further.

B. WEIGHT REDUCTION:

The next area where you can improve is reducing your weight (if you are overweight). This also affects your happiness in life and may astonish you! Over half of

Improving Your Appearance Quotient (AQ)

Americans are overweight. My wife and I are both overweight. People have told us story after story how they were discriminated against based on being overweight. Our America On-line Writer's message box was full of stories relating to appearance discrimination based on weight. We were horrified, but not particularly surprised. Overweight persons suffer terrible mental anguish in the form of teasing and harassment from children and adults, exclusion from jobs, promotions and certain social circles, and even outright hatred at times by other adults. Research points to horrible consequences of being overweight. Tom Cash and Tom Pruzinsky wrote:

> *"Being overweight or obese is a highly stigmatizing condition throughout the life span in our society. When children were asked who they liked best among pictures of peers with various physical handicaps, the obese child was chosen last." (based on research of Richardson, Goodman, Hastorf, & Dornbusch in 1961) "Observed that overweight women dated less often, had less dates or mate satisfaction, and experienced more peer criticism than overweight men or normalweight men and women." (based on research of Stake and Laurer). The stigmatic stereotyping of overweight persons may adversely effect their educational opportunities"*

(based on work of Canning & Mayer in 1966).

A recent Sally Jessey Raphael episode featured an overweight mother being mentally tortured by her children about her overweight condition. They called their mother "piggy", "fat slob", "disgusting." While this is may be an extreme case, many milder forms of fat "bashing" occur regularly. We sat down with 3 other couples and came up with the following names they've heard throughout their life regarding overweight persons:

Comment/Name	Circumstance
1) "Fat Whale"	Heavy Women Cutting in Line at a supermarket
2) "##!!@&&# Fat Slob"	Heavy man driving slowly on a one lane road
3) "She ought to be ashamed" "How ridiculous"	Heavy women in a bathing suit dancing on the front of a boat on a lake
4) "Fat Tub of Lard"	Children picking on a heavy-set child for no apparent reason
5) "Little Porker"	Children's verbal attack on an overweight child after making a common mistake during a game

APPEARANCE IS EVERYTHING

While rude comments might have been forthcoming in some of the above instances, the fact that the person was overweight made them a more convenient and easier target for abuse. Their overweight condition made it easy to attack directly at the heart of their pain center. Focusing on their weight was the easy way to attack a known sensitivity and "get back" at some wrongdoing. If the person were not overweight, the attack might have been quite different or not present at all. Verbal attacks on people's weight are convenient methods to gain dominance over the one attacked. The way overweight people are perceived goes a long way in explaining how they are treated by others. The same couples provided the following key words when describing an extremely overweight person (we asked them to be totally honest):

1) LAZY
2) SLOW
3) UNPRODUCTIVE
4) UNHEALTHY
5) SLOPPY
6) NOT HYGIENIC
7) STUPID (must be to let themselves get that overweight)
8) UNATTRACTIVE
9) BLOBBY
10) NOT SEXY
11) SMELLY
12) MEAN
13) UNINTERESTING
14) RIDICULOUS
15) LACKS FRIENDS
16) FEEL SORRY FOR
17) SHORT LIFE EXPECTANCY
18) NEEDS HELP
19) UNHAPPY
20) MENTALLY PAINED

These words and phrases directed towards overweight people all tend to be very negative. If you are something less than very overweight, then a percentage of the above thoughts/comments probably apply to you. By reducing your weight, you can effectively eliminate the chance of being perceived in light of the above comments. Simply put, persons with a proportionate frame/weight ratio are afforded more positive thoughts than those listed above.

We asked the same persons to give their thoughts and comments about a person with neutral body tone, perfectly matched (subjective, based on their own paradigms) between body frame and weight (i.e. not overweight in their opinion). We developed the following list:

WORDS/THOUGHTS ON NON-OVERWEIGHT PERSON

1) NORMAL
2) WELL ADJUSTED
3) HAPPY
4) HEALTHY
5) FRIENDLY
6) AGILE
7) PUT-TOGETHER

The astonishing thing about this exercise was that fewer comments and thoughts surfaced about the non-overweight (normal) person. When asked about the overweight person, they seemingly went on and on with various thoughts and comments. For the non-overweight person, we noted just the first 3 comments before I had to "prod" for more adjectives. The take-away from this exercise was that the fictitious overweight person had many more presumed negative traits and attributes, while the non-overweight person had positive or neutral attributes, with very little to "pick" or "comment" on. This is consistent with the general tendency to "pick" on overweight persons as noted in Appearance Rule #39.

Appearance Rule #39

An overweight person IS TYPICALLY ASSUMED to have negative personality traits as compared to a non-overweight person. An overweight person generally receives LESS FAVORABLE treatment than does a non-overweight person.

Proofs for Appearance Rule #39:

1. What would be your first reaction if your son/daughter, who is mildly overweight or normal weight, brought home a date whom was well over 400 pounds and introduced them as their new boyfriend/girlfriend? Would you encourage this relationship to continue? Would you be embarrassed? I wouldn't be too pleased since I know the grief they would both be put through!

2. You are walking down the aisle of an airplane and see many attractive, normal weight persons. You then see a person that weighs over 350 pounds sitting alone in a row of 2 seats. You check your ticket—it is the one next to this person! The flight is over 8 hours long. What would your reaction be? I would be upset for many reasons, if not alone for the simple fact that this person would be overflowing their seat space and cramping my side! Although this is a fictitious situation, the reaction is totally honest and based on personal experience.

3. What would be your reaction to a very overweight person loading up their plate at an "all-you-can-eat" buffet? You probably would think, as did we, that this person is gluttonous, "that's how they got that way", and might even be a little annoyed.

I'll bet your reaction would be somewhat different if a thin was in line loading up their plate. You would probably say, as we do, "Gee! I wish I could eat like that and still stay that thin, look so good", etc..

4. What about overweight people on the beach wearing revealing bathing suits. Think of heavy women with "thongs" on or men with huge beer bellies. Many people we talked to feel TOTALLY DISGUSTED by such people.

Another side effect of weight reduction is the change in your perceived age. In writing this book, we noticed a direct correlation between a person being overweight and their perceived age. Overweight persons were consistently rated as being older than their non-overweight counterparts. My wife and I, as overweight persons ourselves, are usually thought to be older than our real ages. The extra weight an overweight person carries around tends to "bloat" their face and cause them to appear much older than their real age.

Weight reduction can have a significant positive effect toward improving your appearance and the way others treat you. The positive effects can be greatly enhanced when the weight reduction is combined with muscle toning as mentioned in section A above. The benefits to facial appearance, body appearance, positive presence (outward attitude and psychological), and positive health effects make exercise and weight reduction a true "win-win" situation. How many other activities can you name which have so many positive, simultaneous effects? Since writing this section, my wife and I started a regular exercise program and have lost 10 pounds combined. We're sick and tired of being treated as "second-class citizens." We are "erasing" the negative thoughts directed toward us (being overweight) so we can be treated based on our real value as people.

C. IMPROVED WARDROBE:

Improving your wardrobe can also have profound effects on how you are treated by other people. By wearing more expensive, more stylish clothes, you change the assumptions people make about your success and capabilities. When you wear worn, torn, or dirty clothes, people assume you are unaccomplished, incapable, or have little money. Where you are and what you do determines whether these assumptions will be made about you by others. If, for example, you are gardening, farming, working a construction project, etc., then people would likely not judge you based on your dress. If, on the other hand, you work at in neutral dress environment, say a grocery store, then others who see or talk to you will likely make these assumptions. We compiled two lists based on a the neutral dress environment of a local grocery store, both based on a normal weight person, one dressed in worn clothes, and the other in very stylish clothes.

THOUGHTS/COMMENTS OF PERSON WEARING WORN CLOTHES

1) POSSIBLY LOW INCOME
2) SOMEWHAT UNEDUCATED

3) WORKS AS A LABORER OR SOME OTHER NON-PROFESSIONAL TRADE
4) CAN'T EXERT MUCH EFFORT (at the store)
5) PROBABLY NOT A HYGIENIC PERSON
6) MAY BE DOWN ON THEIR LUCK `
7) MAY BE A MEAN PERSON (child's comment)
8) LAZY
9) DOESN'T SOCIALIZE MUCH
10) NOT SOPHISTICATED/SMALL TOWN MENTALITY

As with the overweight exercise, we had trouble getting comments from people based on the poorly dressed person. People seemed uncomfortable when commenting on this person. They stated that these assumptions about a person might not be true. They often used the words, such as "PROBABLY", "MAYBE", and "POSSIBLY" to describe this person. They were not sure their statement was true for the poorly dressed person, but that had been their experience with other poorly dressed people. Their paradigm was that poorly dressed people were poorer, not clean, less accomplished. Whether or not it was true for our person was irrelevant. The person was judged based on these people's experience with other poorly dressed persons. Our person could have been a CEO of a major corporation, but it was not the EXPERIENCE of the people we questioned. The same persons were asked to judge a very well-dressed person of similar physical characteristics. The following list shows their thoughts and comments:

THOUGHTS/COMMENTS OF PERSON
WEARING EXPENSIVE CLOTHES

1) PROBABLY HAS MONEY
2) LIKELY WELL EDUCATED
3) OWNS THEIR OWN COMPANY OR WORKS AS A PROFESSIONAL
4) ACCOMPLISHED
5) SEXY
6) CLEAN
7) PROBABLY MARRIED WITH NICE CHILDREN
8) FRIENDLY
9) LIKES THE FINER THINGS IN LIFE
10) CARES ABOUT THEIR APPEARANCE
11) TAKES CARE OF THEMSELVES
12) INTELLIGENT

The words people used to describe this well-dressed person were very favorable and more finite than those used to describe the poorly dressed person. Thoughts were more definitive, stating that the person "DOES", "MOST LIKELY", and even "DEFINITELY" possesses some positive attributes. The well-dressed person was definitely afforded a better positive mental image than the poorly dressed person.

The more favorable treatment was also due to the positive thought process behind those persons meeting the well-dressed person.

APPEARANCE IS EVERYTHING

We found many differences in the way people treated us when we dressed well than when we dressed poorly and compiled a list of treatment differences based on being well dressed as compared to poorly dressed. You may have experienced some of the same treatment we have noted. Compare your list to ours and see how many match your own experience. Add to the list in the blanks provided to make the list more personal.

TREATMENT DIFFERENCES BASED ON BEING WELL-DRESSED

1) FASTER SERVICE IN CERTAIN STORES, RESTAURANTS
2) GREATER ATTENTION ON A CAR SALES LOT
3) PERSONS MORE LIKELY TO MAKE CONVERSATION WITH YOU
4) MORE ATTENTION IN THE WORKPLACE
5) MORE LIKELY TO ATTRACT MEMBERS OF THE OPPOSITE SEX
6) ATTRACT ATTENTION IN GENERAL SOCIAL SETTINGS
7) AROUSE ENVY OF OTHERS
8) PROVIDED WITH MORE OPPORTUNITY FOR JOBS
9) TREATED WITH MORE RESPECT (may be a powerful/influential person)
10) RAISE CURIOSITY OF OTHERS OF WHO YOU MIGHT BE AND WHAT YOU DO FOR A LIVING.

(add your experiences to the list)

11) _____

12) _____

13) _____

14) _____

15) _____

As we stated before, the particular social setting determines whether you will be treated differently based on what you wear. You may ask, "When do I know how to dress well and when not to?", or "What rule should I use to determine when to dress well?." This brings us to Appearance Rule #40 which was provides just such a guide.

Appearance Rule #40

Dress in such a way that you WILL NOT feel uncomfortable or inferior to those around you or those you may unexpectedly come in contact with, including those who directly affect your livelihood or chances for success.

Proofs for Appearance Rule #40:

1. How would you feel if you just finished a gardening project and were wearing very muddy clothes. You then went quickly to the supermarket without changing. You meet your boss who is considering you for promotion. Would you feel comfortable or compelled to explain. If you work for a very professional organization, I'll bet you'd either not dress that way or feel compelled to explain (if given the chance)!

2. How would you dress for an interview? Would you try to look your very best and dress the way the you believe the organization expects their top employees to dress? Would you wear worn/torn clothes? Not if you hoped to get the job!

3. You're going to a farming community to talk to some farmers about a piece of machinery related to your company. Would you feel comfortable meeting these folks at some barn or on their farms in your best suit? I would want to change into a nice, flannel shirt. They would likely feel uncomfortable with you wearing a suit anyway!

Basically, people feel most comfortable with other people that look and act like themselves. Suits for professionals, work clothes for laborers, flannels or blue-jeans for home or garden projects, tuxedos for actors, gowns for actresses/models, etc.. Seldom will you find people from opposite ends of the dress spectrum being together (i.e. gowns with work clothes, tuxedos with blue jeans, etc.).

Improving your wardrobe can have profound effects on the way people treat and perceive you. If combined with muscle toning and weight reduction, you may be able to increase your AQ by 1 to 1 1/2 categories!

D. COSMETIC CHANGES:

Many cosmetic changes can improve your (facial) appearance. We point to these options, briefly touching on each and suggesting how they may change the way others perceive you as a person.

1. Dental Hygiene and Orthodontic Work (Teeth Straightened)

According to research performed by Shaw in 1981, the following conclusion was made:

> "While awaiting the outcome of further research in real life settings where true interaction has taken place, it seems reasonable to anticipate that dento-facial anomalies of sufficient severity to mar a child's facial attractiveness may represent an important social disadvantage. Although the magnitude of this handicap is difficult to define in precise terms, the available evidence indicates that parental concern and desire to have such anomalies corrected in their children is well placed."

APPEARANCE IS EVERYTHING

Shaw used the word "handicap" in describing the effects of dental anomalies. Other research (Terry, 1976) noted that the mouth was a critical component to a person's facial appearance.

Research has consistently shown that, since the mouth is one of the first thing others see when meeting you, the lack of clean or straight teeth can severely effect how people respond to and treat you. As with clothes, a less than presentable dental appearance can give you a less sophisticated, and less accomplished, look. Darkened or crooked teeth might lead others to conclude you are a person of limited means, poorly educated, or less than hygienic. Have you ever seen a person dressed up as a hobo/bum or witch for Halloween? Ever see people darkening their teeth to mimic such (less than desirable) characters? In darkening in their teeth, they attempt to portray a poorer (or more frightening) appearance. They also send a message that poor dental appearance is not desirable under normal circumstances, and that such appearance intimidates or scares other people.

Would the same not be true if your teeth were discolored, missing, or crooked? People we talked with, who had less than straight teeth, said other people tended to focus on their dental anomalies rather than making eye contact with them, similar to the way people react when meeting someone with a pronounced facial scar or blemish. Persons with these dental problems said the staring made them feel "very uncomfortable" and "self-conscious." The following excerpt is from a conversation with Pamela, a CPA from a successful accounting firm, regarding her dental appearance:

Pamela was talking to an associate of mine when she found out I was writing this book. She asked many questions about the project. She asked specifically about facial appearance and how it effected the way people are treated. After giving some insights regarding the different ways people are treated, Pamela independently pointed to her own very crooked front tooth and said, "Yes, I know what you mean!" She said although no adult has ever said anything negative, she feels as though she is being looked upon differently. She said once her godson reached out and touched one of her crooked teeth and said, "Why is that like that?" She's also received comments from other children regarding her dental appearance. She strongly believes that these children are innocently asking and commenting on a topic which most adults secretly wonder about yet are uncomfortable asking or talking about since it is considered impolite or inappropriate.

Pamela was really quite brave to share her experience with me. She is a strong-willed person, unafraid of voicing her opinion. Many others may have encountered this form of dental appearance discrimination, yet are not brave enough to talk about it. Appearance discrimination, both from the discriminator and discriminated standpoint, are "taboo" conversation topics and most people feel uncomfortable talking about them. We sincerely thank you, Pamela, for stepping forward and being so (painfully) honest!

Dental appearance improvement is an effective way to shift focus away from your mouth as a "handicap" or "detraction." Depending on how unattractive your dental appearance is, you may want to consider having some form of dental work done to improve the way others treat and view you. Ask the honest opinion of someone like Pamela to determine whether or not you need to improve your (dental) appearance.

2. PROFESSIONAL HAIR COLORING/STYLING

Another way to quickly (and relatively inexpensively) improve your appearance is to have your hair professionally styled and possibly colored. Actors, actresses, politicians, public relations persons, etc., regularly have their hair done professionally. Thousands of hair salons exist across the country which cater to styling and coloring the hair of public persons. The President and First Lady have had personal hair professionals for years and Congress has long had their own barber shop and beauty salon. Most Hollywood studios have their own salons as do many Television stations and even some corporate boardrooms. Hair styling is a multi-billion dollar industry. There are even magazines dedicated to hair care. Why so much emphasis on hair care? What research supports the notion that "hair appearance matters?"

A study conducted by Roll and Verinis in 1971 found that, *"Blonde hair was rated as most valued (kind),. Black hair was rated as most potent (large), and most active(active). Red hair was rated as least valued(unkind), least potent (small), and least active (inactive).* Another study conducted by Pancer and Meindl in 1978 found that *"hair-length and beardedness can have marked effects on impressions of personality." Subjects' perceptions of the long-haired target provide support for the notion that a negative stereotype is associated with this characteristic. Aspects of this stereotypic view, for example, that long-haired individuals lack intelligence or are reckless, are perhaps important causal determinants of such discriminatory behaviors as the reluctance to employ people with long hair in business or industry."*

In a study conducted by Terry and Brady in 1976 it was found that *"the oral region was the most influential component, followed in order by the eyes, hair, nose, and facial structure(shape and complexion)." Their study, when negating the effects of visual correctives being worn, found hair to be the 3rd most important factor in self-ratings one facial attractiveness.*

The following list describes reasons why professional hair styling has advantages over styling your own hair:

APPEARANCE ADVANTAGES OF PROFESSIONAL HAIR STYLING OVER SELF-STYLING

1) PROFESSIONAL STYLIST HAS MORE TRAINING AND EXPERIENCE
2) PROFESSIONAL STYLIST HAS OUTSIDE PERSPECTIVE OF HOW YOU LOOK AND SHOULD LOOK
3) SAVES TIME, ALLOWS MORE TIME TO EXERCISE OR PURSUE OTHER APPEARANCE ENHANCING ACTIVITIES
4) PROFESSIONAL STYLIST HAS BETTER TOOLS
5) IF A PROFESSIONAL STYLIST MAKES MISTAKES, THEY OFTEN OFFER TO RE-DO YOUR HAIR AT NO CHARGE
6) PROFESSIONAL STYLIST MORE LIKELY KNOWS THE "IN LOOK"
7) A PROFESSIONAL STYLIST CAN MORE EASILY VIEW YOUR ENTIRE LOOK (ON TOP, BEHIND YOU, SILHOUETTE, ETC.) THAN YOU CAN VIA A MIRROR.

Even if you can't afford a professional stylist on a regular basis, you should go periodically to get new ideas (i.e. use the stylist as a consultant). Ask questions while you are there so you may later employ the knowledge when you return to self-styling. In this manner the professional hair stylist helps keep you up with the latest styles, colors, etc., and may correct any mistakes you've have been made while self-styling. Professional hair styling can make another (huge) difference in the way people view and treat you on a daily basis.

3. PROFESSIONAL MAKEUP CONSULTATION:

Like professional hair styling, a professional makeup consultation can provide invaluable insights regarding makeup. The same reasoning applies for professional makeup application as for professional hair styling. The professional makeup consultant has more experience, a broader perspective, more tools and makeup, and most likely a better light "environment" to apply the makeup than you have at home. Unless you work in television or some other form of entertainment, professional makeup consultants should be used (infrequently) to gain additional knowledge, keep up with latest styles, learn new techniques, and catch mistakes made from applying your own makeup.

Research has shown that professional makeup application can have profound effects toward how people perceive you. In 1980, researchers Graham and Jouhar found a correlation between the use of makeup and a higher rating in facial attractiveness. In 1981, these researchers also found that, when females had makeup professionally applied, they were rated as more "socially interesting", "confident", and "secure", which suggested (to them) that "make-up enhances evaluation of the more outgoing aspects of personality." Graham and Jouhar also thought there may exist a "positive cosmetic stereotype which carries its own concept 'what has been cared for is good.'" Another pair of researchers, Miller and Cox, suggested that the degree of makeup usage may act as a cue to "a woman's values, sexual desires, availability."

Today, a multi-billion dollar cosmetic industry exists to manufacture and distribute cosmetics. The acceptability and use of makeup throughout the world has been increasing for years. The person who uses no makeup increasingly finds themselves in a rebellious or non-conformist minority. While individual choices are respected, it may be prudent to apply makeup in certain instances where that extra advantage or appeal may be required (i.e. work, business meetings, weddings, special occasions, etc.). The smart application of makeup is yet another easy way to put another "notch" in your personal appeal "belt."

4. CONTACT LENSES/STYLISH EYEGLASSES

Research abounds on the topic of ocular appearance. In 1970, researchers Terry and Zimmerman argued that "It is generally assumed that social rejection is anxiety-inducing, and thus, a spectacle image, itself, which connotes social rejections, should be anxiety inducing. We reasoned that wearing spectacles leads to the formation of a negative, spectacle image, which is anxiety inducing, and that contact lenses contribute to a reduction of anxiety." They found that contact lens wearers felt anxious when asked to wear spectacles *In 1976, researchers Terry and Kroger wrote "The replacement of framed eye glasses with contact lenses has had dramatic positive psychological effects for* many people, whereas the reintroduction of framed glasses to wearers of contact lenses in a social context is anxiety-producing. Wearing framed eye glasses thus appears to be associated with negative social reactions from other persons." Another study (G. Thornton 1943, 1944) found that persons with glasses were rated higher in honesty, dependability, industriousness, and intelligence.

Still more research points to a dichotomy when spectacles are valued as appearance enhancers. In terms of a person's general appearance, research indicates that spectacles are viewed as not attractive. To persons dealing or working with intellectuals, spectacles might be image enhancing. Many persons in the television industry tend to wear contact lenses versus eyeglasses because they feel that eyeglasses detract from general appearance. How many soap-opera stars can you name who wear glasses? Usually the roles of older/wiser persons have eyeglasses as part of the character's wardrobe. On the other hand, persons associated with intellectual endeavors like engineering wear spectacles on a regular basis without concern. These people are generally less sensitive than television professionals as to their ocular appearance. It is likely that many of their engineering peers wear eyeglasses and that it is informally acceptable. Depending on how sensitive you are to your own appearance, the environment you operate (work) in, and what you're trying to accomplish, you may consider wearing contact lenses versus eyeglasses. In rare and extreme instances (sales to engineering firms or universities, court dealings, etc.), you might even consider wearing clear lens glasses to appear more intellectual, more honest, or more dependable.

What about eye color and colored contact lenses you might ask? Research in this area consists of two significant studies. Researchers Jones and Moyel subjects indicated they considered more friendly the faces that had light, rather than dark, irises (as appearing in black and white photographs). Another pair of researchers, Feinman and Gill (1978), found females to prefer men with dark-colored eyes and males to prefer women with light-colored eyes. The people we asked confirmed these findings, with men stating 82% of the time that they preferred women with blue or green eyes and women we asked confirmed a preference for the dark-eyed men 68% of the time! Based on such findings, you might consider changing your eye color via colored contact lenses. While certainly much less an appearance factor your mouth, weight, hair, and body tone, changing eye color via contact lenses is a relatively easy step you can take to improve your appearance.

5. TANNING AND SKIN CARE:

Many people equate a tan complexion to a healthy or sexy appearance. Many people literally spend hours at the beach, in their backyards, or tanning salons, to gain that "bronze" look. While increasing evidence suggests that the sun's (ultraviolet) rays are actually harmful (can even lead to cancer), it has not slowed the sunbathing masses in search of that "golden brown" appearance. Many people have added sun block lotion to their routine to (presumably) negate the sun's harmful effects, but it does not generally seem to have put a large dent in the overall number of sun bathers. Many men and women we spoke to preferred persons of the opposite sex with darker complexions over a paler person and we asked them why. Their answers are listed below:

APPEARANCE IS EVERYTHING

REASONS DARKER COMPLEXIONS ARE PREFERRED

1) They are sexier
2) They look healthier
3) They seem more mysterious
4) They seem warmer and more friendly

While having some positive appearance effects, one should take the utmost care to not damage the skin when tanning and negate the positive effects of enhanced color. Skin cancer can be gruesome and, in its most severe form, can repulse people from the visible damage and weathered appearance. Be careful!! The temporary gains of bronze color can all be erased by PERMANENT AND GROTESQUE SKIN APPEARANCE!

Skin care in other forms is also very important in maintaining an overall healthy appearance. Clear, unblemished skin was often a quality retained by the ancient Greek Goddesses, and also connoted a healthy person. The use of skin cream, periodic professional facial treatment, and the use of skin-enhancing soaps, can all improve facial appearance. Moisturizing creams, lotions, and gels also have been proven to enhance facial appearance. The adding of moisture to the skin somehow enhances the skin's appearance. We noticed some correlation between the region of the United States where people live and skin clarity. When we were in Mississippi, where the (bathing) water supply is particularly soft and the air tends to be constantly humid, we noticed the clarity and suppleness of people's skin to be much greater than were we lived (central New York with much lower humidity, harder water supply, and much more severe winters). An old women who had lived there a long time told us she believed the combination of high humidity and soft water was "easy on the skin" and added to its appearance. She went on to say (almost in jest) "Why do you think the women are so beautiful in the South and so many Miss America winners have come from southern states?" Whether scientific evidence support this hypothesis remains unknown, but there may some truth to this lady's words. Skin care, via an array of methods, goes a long way to looking healthier, younger, and purer of heart.

6. MANICURE

A professional manicure is another small way you can improve your appearance. It can add that small touch (to your appearance) for that special occasion, public appearance, or significant business meeting/engagement. People we talked to said that a manicure is something only the "well off" would add to the list of personal appearance enhancements. A manicure can then be the perfect added touch, if you have followed the other improvement suggestions in this chapter and want to appear "perfect" or very "affluent" and have them wondering "Who is this person!!"

E. PERSONAL APPEAL:

While not directly related to your appearance, the way you present yourself after people have judged your appearance as acceptable or tolerable can have a profound effect on the way people mentally perceive you. Once someone has been judged one their external appearance, they are subsequently judged on their intelligence, kindness, openness, honesty, and other characteristics. Being viewed as having an "acceptable" appearance is like "getting your foot in the door" for a job interview. Being judged as acceptable in personality is like being perceived able to perform the job after a successful interview. This secondary personality judgment, along with a primary judgment on appearance, form the total opinion of you as a person.

Appearance Rule #41

People first judge you by YOUR APPEARANCE, then your personality, if time and opportunity permit. The longer your exposure to another person, the greater your chance of being judged on personality traits versus appearance alone.

Proofs for Appearance Rule #41:

1. Ever know a woman who was not initially attracted to a man and refused to go out with him but, as the male persisted and was exposed to the female for longer periods of time, she "gave in" and went with the male? They dated for a while or even married? The (female's) secondary personality judgment won out over the primary attractiveness judgment.

2. Ever meet someone who looked real "nerdy" or "dorky?" You then spoke to the person and realized they were intelligent, even eloquent, and very interesting? You find them "neat" to be around and enjoyed their company? Again, the secondary personality judgment is at play. Isn't this the way people should really be judged?

3. Ever pass someone in the mall and think (to yourself), "this person is homely or ugly?" Since your exposure was limited, the person never got a second chance to judge further. This goes on every day, and is most unfortunate. In our "hurry up", instant world, quick summary judgments are becoming more and more the norm.

Even very attractive persons can be thought of as undesirable, ugly, or unappealing, if they lack personal appeal and personality.

REAL LIFE STORY ON AN ATTRACTIVE FEMALE THAT MANY PEOPLE "THOUGHT OF" AS AN UGLY PERSON

The case in point involves a female I used to work with, whom I'll name Kate. Kate was a single, very attractive female (nice complexion, large bosoms, athletic) in an environment with very few men. You'd think the men would have "flocked" to Kate, and that she'd be awash in endless dating opportunities (based on her appearance).

This was, indeed, true when Kate first joined the company or when new men were hired. Kate, in addition to being attractive, was very self-centered and would do just about anything (be it ethical or unethical) to further her position. She was been known to "back-stab", lie, cheat, and literally steal work away from others, to "build" her position at the expense of co-workers. Once people experience this behavior firsthand, they started commenting negatively about Kate. Many people thought very poorly of her "maneuvering", often saying she was "mean", or at times, an "ugly" person. Kate dated many people, but these persons quickly moved on after a short period of time. I had an occasion to ask one person Kate dated why they didn't "hit it off." He said that Kate was real "into herself" and he was not attracted to someone so "into themselves." Being someone who has an "Achilles heel" when it comes to large female bosoms, I should have been naturally attracted to Kate. As a matter of fact, I was very attracted to her for the first week after I joined the company. This appearance attraction (primary judgment) quickly faded when I found out what the true Kate was like (secondary judgment). I now perceive Kate as a mean person, one who is not at all appealing!

The story of Kate is not isolated. I bet you could tell many such a story of an attractive manipulator, or attractive, but mean, person. These people are inarguably (outwardly) attractive yet they lack some personality component that makes them very unattractive persons in the way they are treated by society after maybe a brief attraction based on their external appearance. So people can be both physically attractive yet undesirable and shunned by others in much the same manner as unattractive persons.

Appearance Rule #42

VERY ATTRACTIVE persons who possess negative personality characteristics (i.e. mean, manipulative, pushy, etc.) ARE LIKELY to experience similar negative treatment by society as that experienced by unattractive persons.

Proofs for Appearance Rule #42:

1. You asked an attractive person for a date since "you thought he was cute" or "she was gorgeous." After dating a few times, you find out they are less than honest, mean in nature, or compulsive liars. Would you date these people anymore? Not unless you like liars or mean people. You would tend to avoid this person as "unattractive", if you are like most people.

2. Ever meet an attractive, fast-talking, aggressive car salesman who pushes and pushes to make the sale? You mentally view these smooth talkers as "swindlers", "shysters", or "unethical." Even though the person may be attractive, you want to avoid them. Their physical attractiveness is far outweighed by their negative personality characteristics. You tend to react (toward this person) by avoiding them. The avoidance treatment is generally the same as that experienced by physically unattractive persons.

Your next question may be, "How can I improve my presence and the way people think of me as a person?" The answer lies in an array of methods which we "prescribe" to improve your general appeal.

1. VOCABULARY AND SPEECH IMPROVEMENT

A person who can speak eloquently, and has good command of their vocabulary, has command of their audience. Many schools and classes are available to help people learn to speak clearer, with better content, and with more varied style. Good public speakers generally have participated in some form of speech improvement activities. Clubs such as Toastmasters, help people become better speakers. Any form speaking in front of other people helps improve your ability to speak. Getting over those "jitters" comes from frequent exposure and practice. If you never stumble in front of people, you'll never get to polish and improve your speaking skills.

Even if you're unattractive, people enjoy listening to a good speaker and will be much more receptive to meeting and talking with you. Any person able to speak well will command an audience and more likely be judged on factors other than (their) appearance. If you have improved upon your appearance as prescribed earlier in this chapter, and you improve your public speaking skills, then you've greatly enhance your chances for success in life!

2. EDUCATION

The more you know, the more interesting you become. The command of knowledge and world events makes you that much more interesting a person to be around. By simply reading a daily newspaper or studying about a particular area of interest or curiosity, you have a better chance of participating in, or leading, a conversation. "Knowledge is power", and so it is when speaking to, and interacting with, other people. An intelligent person is far more valuable in many social and business circles than one whom is merely "attractive." Many tribal societies revere the wise man, who is the most knowledgeable, and whom can solve problems regardless of their appeared difficulty. Any chance you get to further your education is yet "another notch in your value belt." Regardless of your appearance, many educated, mature, and older persons will more likely judge you on your intellectual prowess versus your appearance (the reason behind this was covered in chapter 5).

3. DISPOSITION—SMILE!

A person judged to be ugly based on personality usually is done so based on a "nasty" or "mean" disposition. A pleasant disposition and ready smile go a long way in making others comfortable and happy to be around you. A frown of unhappy countenance will have people thinking something is wrong with you (i.e. angry, troubled, mean, unfriendly, etc.). You will likely be avoided and people will not want to be in your company, regardless of your appearance. A conscious effort to improve they way you treat and greet people can go a long way toward having others view you as "attractive" and pleasant to be around. Their secondary personality judgment will far surpass any initial appearance judgment they may have made about you.

4. POSTURE, POISE, ETIQUETTE

The way you carry and "handle" yourself can also add to your mental appearance. Persons who walk, sit, and act with confidence and style are noticed in a positive way.

Persons who walk without style (strut, shuffle, pigeon-toed, or duck-toed), sit without style (slouching, hunched over, leaning), or who display poor manners, are also noticed, but mostly for negative reasons. I have a friend who is very attractive, but slouches a lot when sitting. This slouching gives them the appearance of lacking self-confidence or as coming from a poor upbringing according to our mutual friends. When this behavior was pointed out, my friend said, "Gee, I never thought about that!" Since we do these actions every day, they are part of our subconscious and are not examined very often, if at all. By simply raising our consciousness of our actions, we can change our behavior for the better!

There are schools and books dedicated to helping in this area which we call appearance "etiquette." Another way to improve in this area is to ask friends how you "come across" to others in terms of how you walk, sit, and perform various actions. Work on improving any negative behavior tendencies they may point out. It only takes a couple weeks of conscious effort to change bad habits (really). You will enhance your (AQ) position by not having the way you walk, sit, or act be the topic of (negative) conversation.

5. ASSERTIVENESS WITH STYLE

Some people are just unassertive in dealing with others. Particularly if you unattractive, you should be more assertive and gain the spotlight usually "reserved" for the more attractive. Being politely assertive is a skill that is learned over a long period of time. You want to ensure that you are not labeled as being overly assertive and run the risk of being labeled a "jerk" "hussy" or "smartass." Assertiveness training and books are becoming increasingly available and should be the primary source for improving your assertiveness. Unfortunately, increasing your assertiveness contradicts some of our teachings as children, namely "Speak when spoken to", "wait your turn", "don't butt in", etc.. While these axioms are still good advice, being assertive means making sure you get your turn and making sure you're allowed into the conversation (at some point). More aggressive people are typically respected since they are viewed as "fighters" for their particular position or cause. Persons who stand quietly on the sideline will never be "known" and never able to reveal their true self and secondary personality characteristics. In Japan, people are taught "to say it loud and with conviction, even if what you are saying is dead wrong." While we would not go that far, stating your position in a strong and clear voice goes a long way in gaining the attention and respect of others, regardless of your appearance!

F. COSMETIC SURGERY:

Another physical appearance improvement suggestion is to undergo cosmetic surgery. There are many types of surgery that can help you "jump start" on your appearance. Cosmetic surgery is usually a quick fix, but can many times be very expensive. Due to the intrusive nature of these procedures, there may be negative side-effects. Check with your doctor before undergoing any of these procedures. We'll simply list the different types of cosmetic surgery available and the (potential) benefit for each.

Improving Your Appearance Quotient (AQ)

1. FACE-LIFT/PLASTIC SURGERY:

Face-lifts are used to tighten the facial muscles and give the face a less baggy or "sleeker" appearance. Similar benefit can be gained by long term exercise. A face-lift is a quicker method for achieving this result.

2. LIPOSUCTION

Liposuction procedures are used to remove excess fat and cellulite. The procedure literally "sucks" the fat from your body in much the manner a vacuum cleaner would clean Jello from a bag. The same benefit can be obtained via weight reduction and regular exercise.

3. NOSE REDUCTION

Reducing the size of one's nose cannot be obtained via any method other than surgery. Many people have successfully underwent this type of surgery without risk. My sister-in-law had this procedure done a few years ago with no side-effects. You actually get to "pick" a new nose from a book in much the way you would piece together a composite sketch to identify a criminal. The reduction of a large nose can have a great effect toward enhancing your appearance. No more "Pinnochio" jokes or other snide comments behind your back!

4. BLEMISH/WART REMOVAL

Blemish and wart removal can have small, but positive effects on your appearance and are relatively inexpensive. Warts connote ugliness and are often associated with witches at Halloween. Wart removal should be considered particularly if the warts are visible and detract from your facial appearance. Warts seen only when wearing a bathing suit, or seen only by a husband/wife or bed partner are a matter of personal choice and preference. Discuss the matter with a doctor and determine whether they make you feel uncomfortable. As a general rule, if they make you uncomfortable, consider removing them.

Blemish removal can also enhance your appearance by negating a blemished "look." Blemishes connote damage for the person in the same manner they do for fruit at the supermarket. Some people may like their appearance, but few people we asked thought them to be appealing.

5. BREAST ENLARGEMENT:

Female breast enlargement can enhance the size and shape of the breasts. Many women in the exotic dance business have this procedure done to increase their income. Other women who are very sensitive to their appearance also had this operation done. There has been much discussion about the safety of this procedure. If you absolutely have to have this procedure done, please check with several doctors and read up on it. A temporary improvement in breast size, is not worth any health risk!

CHAPTER 7 SUMMARY

A. There are many ways to improve your appearance via your own actions.

B. Improving muscle tone can change the shape and contour of your face to appear more attractive.

C. Weight reduction can drastically improve the way people treat you and reduce the chance that you will be criticized.

D. Dressing better in more expensive clothes can make you seem more intelligent, accomplished, and more well-to-do.

E. Dressing in unappealing clothes is risky and can give others a very negative reaction to you.

F. Cosmetic changes taken together can have a profound positive effect on your appearance.

G. Poor appearance of teeth, hair, mouth, or eyes can bring negative reaction from others you meet.

H. Professional hair styling and cosmetic application can have advantages over maintaining hair/cosmetics yourself.

I. Persons who tan or generally take care of their skin are considered sexier, healthier, and more "mysterious" than those who do not.

J. A person if FIRST judged by their appearance then by personality factors.

K. The longer a person is exposed to others, the more likely they will be judged by personality factors versus appearance factors.

L. Even very attractive persons can be considered "ugly" or "unappealing" if they are severely lacking in personality.

M. An improvement in personality and general appeal can be accomplished via multiple methods.

N. An improvement in personality and general appeal can improve the way people view you and how (mentally) attractive you are.

O. Many different cosmetic surgery procedures are available for appearance "quick-fixes."

P. Cosmetic surgery can have negative side-effects and should only be undertaken after much consultation and self-research.

CHAPTER
8

WHAT IS WRONG WITH BEING AVERAGE!

A. The Law of Appearance Averages

As opposed to those we see appearing daily on television commercials, in soap operas, and as TV news "anchors", most people in society are less attractive and more average in appearance. For example, most people are not super models with perfect body weight, perfectly coiffured hair and makeup application, or display a perfect complexion. People, on average, also don't look like the models we see "selling" clothes, bathing suits, makeup, etc. in any of the fashion or other magazines such as GQ, Self, Glamour, Cosmopolitan, etc., etc., etc..

This excerpt from the book, Body Images, reveals some startling research:

> *"Communications media socialize the attractiveness stereotypes by associating good looks with a glamorous life, thus creating an insidious contrast effect. After exposure to highly attractive media models, self-rating of appearance drops (Cash, Cash, and Butters, 1983) and ratings of other people's appearance declines as well (Kenrick & Gutierres, 1980). Carefully contrived advertisements compress standards of attractiveness into a young, idealized extreme that is virtually unattainable."*

What effect does this constant mass media exposure to those who are unrepresentative of average society have on our day-to-day lives? Why is the majority of society those of average appearance discriminated against by a minority and a supporting media establishment? What message is subconsciously sent (and received) by our exposure to those deemed "beautiful", but who are a far cry from Mr. or Ms. "average" citizen? What appearance trends have been set by the media, and what societal appearance stigmas, both positive and negative, exist today? This chapter attempts to answer these questions and reveal where we are headed as a society in terms of appearance discrimination.

B. Negative stigma of being less than attractive or
average in appearance

1. Societal Trends during the 20th Century
The concept of what is beautiful and attractive has never remained constant as it has changed many times and, rather dramatically. In the late 19th Century in the United States, many women worried about being too thin. Society cherished the buxom, wide-hip look. Women frequently used padding to bolster their size and wore bristles to make their buttocks appear larger. Physicians (during this period) encouraged people to maintain larger frame weight since it was believed to be healthier. Paintings, sculptures, and models were mostly of large proportions, what we would call "plump" today. The best known landmark from this time is the Statue of Liberty standing in New York Harbor. It is a large framed, rounded figure, which would likely earn the name "fat", "rotund", or "plump" today. In the 1880's, this look was considered the epitome of beauty and attractiveness. Women (or men) who could afford to eat and avoid manual labor in their labor-intensive world were envied. These (plumper) people were the elite, the pampered, the wealthy, the attractive. They were unique, since they were typically the only ones who could afford to be heavier by not partaking in labor-intensive jobs!

The start of the 19th Century was also the beginning of the industrialization of America. Along with less time and labor-intensive jobs, went the exclusivity and uniqueness of being "weightier" due to wealth and the ability to avoid "working out" during the course of doing one's job. It was also around the turn of the 20th century that we started seeing the "fall from grace" of the heavier woman as the model of beauty. The beauty model (for women) became those with large breasts, somewhat taller, somewhat thinner, and, for the first time in history, women with shapely legs. Women who were deemed respectable had never shown their legs in public before this time. In the early 1900's, women's clothes became baggier and hemlines much higher than in the past. Flat-chested "flappers", as they called them, were the model of beauty and appeared almost boy-like in nature. Women went on starvation diets, used rolling pins to flatten their stomachs and hips, and strenuous exercise became the norm for many. The Ladies Home Journal first debuted during the 1920's and provided the first glimpse of what was "beautiful" for many upper and middle income people.

During the 1930's, the beauty standard changed again. "Large" was back in for many women and the "big breast" movement started. Waistlines were relaxed and long-legged, busty women were the model of beauty. One of the most popular figures from this period was Betty Grabel, who was renowned for her tight "buns" and what were called at the time her "million dollar legs." Lana Turner and Jane Russell were introduced as the "sweater girls", and they had larger breasts than most models of the previous era (1920's). This was the first time that Miss America Pageant winners had breast sizes larger than their hip measurements, unheard of during the early 1900's!

The 1950's and 1960's saw yet more changes on the beauty scene. The trend of idolizing large-breasted women continued as Playboy magazine highlighted the large-breasted woman with the busty Marilyn Monroe having the distinction as the first Playboy "centerfold" model. During the 50's, women's waist size declined as both large breasts and larger hips were highlighted. The 1960's started the "thin is in" movement with the appearance of a model named Leslie Hornby Armstrong from England. Nicknamed "Twiggy", this 97 pound, "sexy" model started the trend toward more slender, leaner models. During the same period, obstetricians advocated strict diets to pregnant women and permitted only very low weight gain by expectant mothers. From this point forward in history, the trend has been pretty constantly downward in terms of waistlines, weight, and body proportions. It was found by Freedman in 1986, that Playboy centerfolds have "grown" slimmer every year since the magazine began. Mazur, in 1986, found that, while the breast size has remained constant and more toward the larger size, Playmates have become taller, thinner, and displayed less distinguishable hips!

C. The Role of the Media in Defining Beauty

The mass media has completely transformed the way it operates over the years. Early in our century, it was limited in both coverage and broadcast area. Reporters covered events by reporting what they saw at face value as opposed to today's "behind the scenes", "in-depth" reports. Commercials and fashion magazines were few, models and sports stars were seldom used in advertisements, and Miss America pageants were not televised. Today's media has a profound effect at how we look at ourselves and how beauty is defined. An excerpt from the book, The Social Psychology of Facial Appearance, portrayed the media as follows:

> *"Media advertising of beauty aids, for example, may accelerate the process that attractive people have better prospects for happy professional and social lives. The fetish of beauty encouraged by advertising may persuade the public as to the desirability of possessing a face with perfect contours and fresh skin, with rows of shinning teeth. Beauty is presented as the promise of complete satisfaction by purchasing the product in question, the public can identify with the attractive, "contented" people in the advertisements. As the cosmetic industry expands, advertisements on TV, radio, billboards, and magazines become more and more sophisticated, emphasizing the need to be aware of and to control appearance. The boom in the cosmetic industry, plastic surgery, diet foods, and the fashion business are all indicators of the major economic investment made in appearance."*

And on the topic of television, The Social Psychology of Facial Appearance contained the following passage:

> *"In the United States, television viewers are subjected to the same message again and again-beautiful*

> *people posses material goods, are loved, usually find*
> *success and happiness, and are worshipped from afar.*
> *Thus television advertisements can act as the "hid-*
> *den persuader", filling our screen with beautiful peo-*
> *ple. Commercials use sophisticated techniques in*
> *attempts to manipulate viewers into wanting cer-*
> *tain products."*

In The Social Psychology of Facial Appearance, it was reported that a researcher (Tan, 1979) had a group of high school students view over a dozen television commercials stressing how important it is to be beautiful and another group of students not view these commercials. Tan found that the group that viewed the commercials more likely to agree with statements such as "beauty is personally desirable for me" and "beauty is important to be popular with men."

The above passages and research led us to the formulation of the next appearance rule.

Appearance Rule #43

The more a person is exposed to media portraying atypical, beautiful people, the MORE LIKELY that person will become more self conscious, discouraged, angry, or withdrawn because they fail to appear similarly attractive.

Proofs for Appearance Rule #43:

1. How would you think an extremely overweight and basically unattractive person would feel after watching soap operas and commercials full of gorgeous men and beautiful women? Many people I talked to feel jealous, inadequate, and like they "missed the boat" in terms of having "it all." What about you? How do these people make you feel? Are these people anything like your neighbors, friends and acquaintances in terms of appearance?

2. Who would you expect to display more self-confidence? Someone who looked exactly like an attractive, sought-after television star, or someone who is far from the beauty "ideal" (i.e. overweight, blemished skin, disproportionate torso, head, and facial features)? The star-like person would probably take every opportunity to be seen in public, while the unattractive person would probably frequently retreat from public view.

As an exercise, we traveled to a local magazine store to see just how many titles were available in a given month on high fashion, appearance, looks, makeup, dating and appearance, etc.. We found the following in about 15 minutes:

Magazines

1. VIE—Health, Beauty, Fitness	24. MUSCULAR
2. TOP HEALTH & BEAUTY	25. FLEX
3. SASSY	26. McCALL'S
4. BEAUTIFUL BRIDES	27. GLAMOUR
5. ALLURE	28. ESQUIRE GENTLEMAN
6. MARIE CLAIRE	29. FOR WOMEN FIRST
7. TOP MODEL	30. WOMAN'S WORLD
8. ELLE	31. VOGUE
9. OK	32. EBONY
10. ELEGANT BRIDE	33. WOMEN'S DAY BEAUTY
11. COSMOPOLITAN	34. UPSCALE '95
12. BRIDAL HAIR	35. VANITY FAIR
13. CELEBRITY HAIRSTYLES	36. AMERICAN CHEERLEADER
14. STAR HAIRDOS	37. YOUR PROM
15. BLACK HAIRCARE	38. DIET AND EXERCISE
16. BIG BEAUTIFUL WOMEN	39. SHAPE
17. SOPHISTICATE'S HAIRSTYLEGUIDE	40. ULTIMATE BODY
18. SHORT HAIRSTYLES	41. NEW BODY
19. YM (YOUNG AND MODERN)	42. TRUE LOVE
20. TOTAL FITNESS	43. TEEN
21. MEN'S FITNESS	44. SELF
22. IRONMAN	45. W (Women)
23. MUSCLES AND FITNESS	

We were also curious to see when these magazines came into existence to determine how long the beauty "bombardment" has been underway. Over 90% of these magazines came into existence after 1968! The slope of the curve of magazines coming into existence appears on Chart 7. Our conclusion is that this media-driven beauty bombardment has increased significantly over the past 20-30 years.

We also looked at articles highlighted in these magazines to see what was "important" and what types of messages were being "drummed" into our heads. The articles were as follows (from this one trip to the magazine store):

Beauty Magazine Articles

1. "HOW TO HAVE A DANCER'S BODY"
2. "SEXY WAISTLINE FOR SUMMER"
3. "SMOOTH THIGHS, SLEEK LEGS, THE NEW WAY TO BEAT CELLULITE"
4. "56 LOOKS YOU'LL LOVE FOR SPRING"
5. "THE 11 MOST COVETED BEAUTY PRODUCTS"
6. "LOOK BETTER NAKED"
7. "SMART HAIR, SEXY MAKEUP"

8. "SUPERMODEL SECRETS—BEAUTY TIPS—WHAT THEY DESIRE, & HOW THEY GET IT"
9. "DIANA TO MADONNA—THE SECRETS OF 10 TOP HAIRSTYLES"
10. "BE THE BRIDE OF YOUR DREAMS"
11. "WORLD CLASS COURTESAN'S SECRETS FOR LANDING WEALTHY, POWERFUL MEN"
12. "CHOOSE YOUR PERFECT BRIDAL STYLE"
13. "SEXY HONEYMOON HAIR"
14. "OVER 250 STUNNING HAIRSTYLES"
15. "50 HOT NEW (HAIR) LOOKS"
16. "SEXY, SOFT, SHINY (HAIR)"
17. "HINTS FOR FINDING YOUR PERFECT STYLE"
18. "HE'S SEXY, HE'S EXCITING, AND HE'S ALL WRONG FOR ME"
19. "SPECIAL HOLLYWOOD ISSUE: EXCLUSIVE PORTFOLIO— 150 STARS. THE POWERFUL AND GLAMOUROUS OF THE MOVIES"
20. "THE 4 PRETTIEST HAIRSTYLES FOR SPRING"
21. "AWESOME CHEER FASHION '95"
22. "ARE YOU TOO THIN?" (watch out if "Madison Avenue" picks up on this)
23. "THICKER, SHINIER HAIR IN 7 DAYS"
24. "5 NEW TRICKS FOR GORGEOUS EYES"
25. "'THE LOOK'—SIMPLE/CHIC"
26. "SEXY HAIR IN 15 MINUTES"
27. "CONFIDENCE BUILDERS FROM HIGH ACHIEVERS"
28. "HAIR—GO FOR GORGEOUS"
29. "WILD WILD WEST—MORE THAN 100 PAGES OF LEADING MEN, BIKINI BEAUTIES, SUPERDUDES AND HOLLYWOOD HEAVIES"
30. "WHY MEN GIVE CERTAIN WOMEN MORE RESPECT THAN OTHERS" (article dealt with appearance differences)
31. "14 (TOP) HAIRSTYLES"
32. "SWIMWEAR ILLUSTRATED—SIZZLING SUMMER STYLES"
33. "BEAUTIFUL GIRLS—IS IT NORMAL TO HATE THEM?"
34. "MY BODY IS SO UGLY" (great self-esteem builder!)
35. "HOW TO LOVE YOUR LOOKS" (converse of #34)
36. "YOUR LOOKS—GET INTO THE PINK" (ditto)
37. "BEAUTY TRADE-OFFS"
38. "GORGEOUS, FIT, AND ENERGETIC AT 48!"
39. "GET A PERFECT COMPLEXION"
40. "HOW THE RICH GET SLIM—YOU CAN TOO"
41. "GLAM GOWNS. SEQUINS, SPARKLE, SHINE"

The messages sent by the above titles is that we all need to improve and look our best to do well in society. In order to "be somebody", we need to look as perfect and strive (in any way possible) to achieve beauty perfection. If we do not strive for beauty perfection, we are considered less than desirable, not beautiful, and thought of as "lazy" for not trying to improve. Another excerpt from the book, The Social Psychology of Facial Appearance, had this to say about women's magazines in particular:

> *"Women's magazines continue to offer advice on how to correct "faults" in appearance, encouraging readers to strive to match up to the glossy images projected by glamorous models. Most of us have a desire to conform to the standards that we believe are the norm for society. A failure to do so sets us apart both in our own estimation, and in the estimation of others. Magazines project images of women with flawless inviting bodies, with young, firm, symmetrical breasts-thus exposing readers to a stereotyped ideal. The idea of "corrective" surgery is introduced, implying that there is a norm from which we have deviated, and that we should strive to correct."*

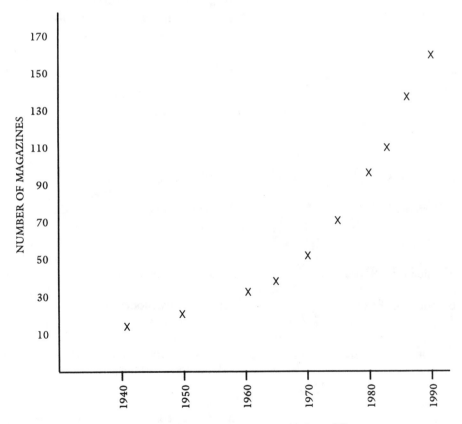

Appearance Magazine In Existence Over Time

Chart 7

APPEARANCE IS EVERYTHING

Maybe the more appropriate message is that we spend in order to account for the multi-trillion dollars in sales of cosmetics, beauty-care services, fashion clothing, cosmetic surgery, etc.. Just think how many ways the beauty "message" reaches us today as compared to years ago. The following is a compilation of media methods for "bombarding" us with the beauty message:

Media	_Presenting_
1. Magazines	* Models
	* Makeover stories
	* Hottest male/females
	* Beauty contests
	* What's hot in fashion
	* Swimsuit issues
	* Centerfolds
2. Television	* Attractive Newspersons
	* Attractive show (co)hosts
	* Attractive persons in commercials
	* Attractive Soap Opera stars
	* Beauty Contests
	* Glamorous award ceremonies
	* "Supermodels"
	* Shows heralding beauty
	(Baywatch, Dallas, Dynasty,
	Designing Women,
	Charlie's Angels, etc.)
3. Billboards	* Models selling products
4. Posters	* Attractive women on Beer posters
	* Models/attractive sports stars
	selling a product
5. Calendars	* Attractive women/men on product calendars
6. Store Displays	* Very attractive models in store
	windows/displays
7. Promotional Videos	* Attractive people selling, explaining,
	or advocating a product
Media	_Presenting_
8. PR Videos	* Attractive people explaining or advocating a
	particular product or presenting a company
	position

9. Sales people   * Attractive sales people selling anything from industrial products to used cars

10. Service personnel   * Attractive waitresses, waiters, hostesses, hosts, performers, etc..

Just think how many ways and times this message reaches us during the course of our daily activities. We see the "beauty factor" countless times each day and subconsciously process these subtle messages.

To better prove the point that the beauty message is extremely pervasive, we changed our routine one weekend and made a conscious log of the "beauty factor" by noting specific indicators. Each time we encountered a "beauty source" from the above list (magazine, television, etc.), we noted the Appearance Quotient of persons we saw from that source (see Chapter 1 for an explanation of AQ). The resulting beauty "factor" gave us a look at how beauty was distributed amongst all the people we saw from each source. One would expect to see an average distribution of attractiveness in magazines, television, billboards, etc., since beauty is distributed fairly evenly throughout society. If not, one would expect some sort of artificial "skewing" to take place. The following is the rather amazing summary of our recorded weekend "adventure":

Source	Number of People Viewed	Number Viewed by Appearance Category
1. Magazines	41	1's—37
		2's—02
		3's—01
		4's—01
		5's—00
2. Television	77	1's—52
		2's—17
		3's—05
		4's—03
		5's—00
3. Billboards	8	1's—06
		2's—02
		3's—00
		4's—00
		5's—00
4. Posters	1	1's—00
		2's—01
		3's—00
		4's—00
		5's—00

5. Calendars	12	1's—12
		2's—00
		3's—00
		4's—00
		5's—00

6. Store Displays	22	1's—18
		2's—03
		3's—01
		4's—00
		5's—00

7/8. Videos	00	1's—00
	(None Seen this weekend)	2's—00
		3's—00
		4's—00
		5's—00

9. Sales people	12	1's—02
		2's—05
		3's—04
		4's—01
		5's—00

10. Service people	27	1's—01
		2's—12
		3's—13
		4's—01
		5's—00

We were quite surprised at our findings, however at this stage of (writing) the book, somewhat less shocked then when we first started performing research. What the (above) numbers show is that there is a "skewing" of numbers toward attractive people in roles dealing with the media and public relations. We would expect to find a bell curve similar to that presented in Chapter 1. Instead, we found the most attractive people in society are continually the most visible. Take magazines for example. A full 90% of people viewed in the magazines we viewed were Category 1's or "beautiful" people. A full 95% of people were "very attractive" and above (Category 1's and 2's). Is this truly representative of America? Are 95% of this country's inhabitants very attractive or beautiful? Calendars were another example. All people viewed (on a particular calendar) were beautiful—a full 100%. Representative? Hardly! The bottom line is that advertising companies believe that "unattractive" or "average" does not sell products! The formula for what is going on with today's media and this artificial skewing of beauty relates to Appearance Rule #44, a sort of logical progression why beautiful people are disproportionately portrayed in the media and virtually show up wherever a media or a public relations related job exists!

Appearance Rule #44

Beauty attracts attention and is pleasant to view. a) Since beauty is pleasant to view, we logically wish to prolong our exposure to, and contact with it, whether it be a person, flower, scenic vista, or other source. b) Since we tend to notice and lock (visually) on to beauty, we're MORE LIKELY we are to focus on the message being brought forth. The message or product then becomes associated with something beautiful and pleasant. c) The beauty source therefore is generally more effective in selling than the unattractive source that may go unnoticed or purposely ignored. d) Beautiful people, therefore, generally sell more effectively and are sought by the media disproportionately more often than average or unattractive people.

Proofs for Appearance Rule #44:

1. When was the last time you saw an unattractive person in a cosmetics or any other beauty product advertisement? How about other products? I can recall only one or two unattractive persons in (any) ads after watching virtually tens of thousands of commercials. Thinking back, these ads focused primarily on comedy or irony to get their point (message) across! Is being attractive an "unwritten rule" of commercials or advertising?

2. Ever see a really attractive man or voluptuous women selling a product on television and find yourself stopping "dead in your tracks" to take explicit notice of the person (and perhaps the product being sold)? I know my wife and I have many times. Would you react the same if an unattractive person were in the same ad? I'll bet not!

The message here is, if you are average, you had better change and conform to the "beauty ideal." You'd better use all your (monetary) resources to acquire "the look" if you want to be anybody. If not, you'll be left "in the dust", unattractive, undesired, second-class!

D. Achievement versus perception

The attractive, as we found previous chapters, are ascribed many positive personality characteristics and assumed capable of greater achievement or higher levels of success than the unattractive. That being true, how does one explain the fact that there are many unattractive millionaires? Did they all win the lottery? Is there some "delta" between the perception of one's ability based on their attractiveness and real accomplishment? Many unattractive people achieve greatness and live their successful, productive, affluent, happy lives. What is their "key" to success? How can a less attractive person "get ahead" and achieve great things?

The answer seems to come from two factors. The first relates to the Life Success Formula we presented in Chapter 4. Appearance is but one of many factors in the formula for success (in life). The stronger a person is in other life success factors such as perseverance, intelligence, education, personality, etc., the less an unattractive appearance must be overcome, and therefore is less relevant. Take an unattractive but extremely intelligent person or one with incredible drive and perseverance. These people have a distinct advantage over all others who are unattractive but whom do not possess the same levels of motivation or intelligence. They may even have an edge over an attractive person who is less intelligent or motivated, depending on what is being attempted. An unattractive, yet intelligent, person would be in a far better position when applying for an engineering or research job than an attractive, less intelligent person.

The second factor is the degree of reliance on internal versus external motivation. If you are externally motivated, you tend to seek out, and need, the approval of others in your attempt to be accepted. If you are unattractive and also externally motivated, you tend to internalize any rejection from others and allow this (rejection) to adversely affect your self-esteem, self-confidence, and level of motivation. Externally motivated people are more easily affected by criticism, ridicule, and rejection than are internally motivated people. Internally motivated people, on the other hand, have strong internal beliefs, faith, and motivations that are virtually impervious from attack by others. These people are analogous to military tanks. They keep going despite rough going (criticism, rejection), being (verbally) fired upon, and are determined to move forward toward their objectives. These internally motivated individuals have very strong beliefs in what is right and what is wrong, and maintain a very specific agenda based on those beliefs. They are not easily influenced or dissuaded. They do not experience low self-esteem, lost self-confidence, or display less motivation when met with rejection or criticism as might the externally motivated person. Ever hear the expression, "he/she won't take no for an answer?"

One person in history who comes readily to mind is Thomas Edison. Here was a very internally motivated person, one who strongly believed in his abilities and was not detracted from his ideas (such as the electric light bulb) when people told him he was "insane" or should stop "wasting time" on such ludicrous ideas. Had Edison been externally motivated, he might never have invented the light bulb! He would have succumbed to outside criticism (in an attempt to conform and be accepted) and lost interest in pursuing his research!

Unattractive, internally motivated people tend to maintain their sense of self-worth, regardless of rejection or criticism by others. These people tend to believe strongly in themselves and move forward toward their goals despite any obstacles or negative influences. Unattractive people who are externally motivated are subject to lost self-confidence, low self-esteem, and lack of motivation via rejection or criticism by other people. Appearance Rule #45 addresses internal versus external motivation when related to appearance.

Appearance Rule #45

People who are both unattractive and externally motivated by criticism, rejection, etc., ARE MORE LIKELY to display less self-confidence, have low self-esteem and lack motivation than will internally motivated, unattractive people.

Proofs for Appearance Rule #45:

1. Ever see someone sulk, act depressed, or become withdrawn after having a fight (argument), being picked on (teased), or being rejected? If so, you witnessed an externally motivated person in action. These people virtually "stew" and internalize the negative events. They either blame themselves or they believe the accuser or rejecter was right in their actions. They actually start to adopt the shortcomings being communicated by others. An unattractive person of this sort would say after a rejection or criticism about their appearance, "Am I really that unattractive?", "Do you think I'm that bad?", or "I wonder if he/she may be right?."

2. Ever see someone laugh, smirk, or even become amused after someone rejected them or attacked them verbally? These people could literally "care less" about what other people think. In fact, they are often amused at the "stupidity" of others for even questioning what they believe to be true. An unattractive person of this nature would say, "I know I have a lot to offer—too bad some people are too stupid to realize it. Oh well, their loss!."

So, "what is wrong with being average?" Nothing at all, as long as you believe in yourself and maintain your self-worth. Accepting yourself as "who you are" is key to this process. Wanting to improve your appearance is perfectly acceptable (and normal), but only if it comes based on your personal motivation as opposed to external influences, particularly criticisms or rejections. Otherwise, you're improving yourself simply to please others rather than yourself. You (unattractive or attractive) can achieve greatness. Just believe in yourself and stop at nothing in achieving your goals. The Healthlines newsletter, published by the Scott Publishing company, had the following interesting insights on this topic in their March 1995 issue (Volume XIII, No. 3):

> "When you look in the mirror do you reduce your identity to a less-than-perfect body part? Big hips, receding hairline double chin... No wonder. We've been fed a steady diet of idealized images of thinness and beauty that are virtually impossible for most of us to achieve or maintain. The fallout from this obsession with perfect bodies is widespread among all ages and sexes...An epidemic in eating disorders. Boys and girls worrying about their bodies and counting calories by age 9. Dramatic increases in cosmetic surgeries. Granted, most everyone would

like to change some feature of his or her looks. But an unhealthy body image can lead to compulsive overeating or fasting, bouts of depression, and a disabling lack of confidence. People who believe their bodies don't measure up often feel they can't measure up in other areas. Don't be hard on yourself. Instead of dwelling on the parts you dislike, study the things that you feel are right about you—your intelligence, generosity, wit and experience as well as your best physical features. When you gaze into the mirror, remind yourself that looking young and thin is not the most important thing in life. And worrying about what you don't have is a waste of time and energy. If you do want to change some things, aim for a healthy body through a sensible diet and regular exercise-not one that conforms to an unattainable image. After all, physical appearance is only part of the package. How you feel about yourself, the strength of your relationships, and your personal growth will sustain you through life far better that the ability to look "perfect" in a bathing suit."

This article, written to alert us to the mental and physical health effects of obsession with one's appearance, adds another insight into the effects of the today's bombardment of beauty ideals. The article also seems to indicate there is absolutely nothing wrong with being average and being yourself. It also points to the very real, negative effects of "trying to be somebody you are not" and cannot become. Knowing the difference can make the difference between being happy and contented or living your life always longing for, but never arriving at, an image that is not you!

Average describes the vast majority of us and a good number of us (average people) are very successful, rich, happy, etc.. The key is not becoming obsessed with appearance and focusing on what you truly want out of life as opposed to attempting to adopt the appearance or goals of the societal "ideal." If you totally accept yourself (including your shortcomings), strive for what you really believe in, cherish your strengths, and maintain an acceptable appearance (to you), you're more likely to be happy and successful. Being "beautiful" has little to do with being happy. As we'll find out, it may actually make you miserable. Attaining beauty, and maintaining it, may actually come at a terrible price for people who become obsessed with "beauty at all costs."

E. Live by the mirror, die by the mirror

Another aspect to consider regarding "what is wrong with being average?" is the opposite "side of the coin." Ask yourself what's wrong with being beautiful? Natural beauty (with little effort to improve or maintain) comes to very few. Those at the opposite end of the spectrum, those who live, breathe, and die beauty improvement, are literally "addicted" to this life-style! Every aspect of these beauty-addicted people, as well as their spouse or "significant other", must be appearance "perfect." Every minute of most every waking hour is spent attempting to maintain or improve appearance. The quest for beauty becomes a life-style in itself with no further goals other than "the body beautiful." These people have been labeled by society and often earn themselves such names as:

1. Shallow
2. Vain
3. Pompous
4. Flashy
5. Self-centered
6. Conceited
7. Skin-deep
8. Cheap
9. Looks Obsessed
10. Hedonistic

The common denominator with most of the above labels is that the person is not based on, or motivated by, deep beliefs or the betterment of others. The term "shallow" was derived from the analogy of the tree where roots of a shallow tree are likely to uproot given the slightest wind. Likewise, shallow people tend to gravitate and "blow" toward the most attractive people or objects. They are not deeply rooted by long-term goals, deep beliefs, or strong convictions. I came across an astonishing story of a married couple regarding the fleeting focus on appearance and shallowness of people that are so beauty-focused. This story was so incredible I still can't get over it today. Ironically, I heard this story told by a woman customer at hair salon to the salon owner. The story details the relationship of a shallow woman who married a once handsome man. The names in this story are fictitious.

Mary married Mike because she was so "attracted" to him. Mike was on the football team, was well built, and had many women "chasing" after him. Mary dated Mike for several years and decided to marry him. Mary thought Mike was a "gorgeous catch" and felt herself so lucky to be with someone so "good looking." Mike and Mary had one child and seemed very happy. Mary was so proud. She had an "adorable" husband and a "beautiful" baby. Mike decided to take a promotion from his company as a salesman. While this meant more money and a better job, it also required being "on the road" for days on end. Mike took the job because weekend travel was non-existent or rare. As the months passed, Mike started gaining weight since he often had to eat out. Mary always spoke of having a second child. After about a year, Mike had gained about 25-30 pounds. Life on the road was "taking its toll." Mary began to make very public and cutting comments about Mike's weight and his appearance. She started to minimize their intimate relations, and basically lost interest in Mike. Mary eventually wouldn't let Mike touch her and filed for divorce. She started dating shortly thereafter, telling her friend, "I want to meet someone else handsome to marry and impregnate me. My biological clock is still ticking. I'll make sure the next one stays fit—no more Mike's."

I was stunned when I heard this story. How shallow can a person be?! The slightest bit of wind (heavier Mike), the shallow person (Mary) was blown away toward the next attractive person to satisfy her twisted and hollow sense of being. People who have friends, marriages, or other relationships with shallow people have to constantly worry that, if their outward person changes, which is much more volatile than the inner person, these friends or lovers will be friends or lovers no longer.

There are many other negative aspects associated with being overly concerned, or obsessed with, attaining ideal beauty. They are:

1. Eating disorders

As the Healthlines article earlier pointed out, eating disorders are a large concern for people wanting to be beautiful and thin. Bulimia and Anorexia are eating disorders on the rise due to people identifying with increasingly thinner models. As the beauty "ideal" has evolved over the years, the weight of models has dramatically reduced. Some sources put the reduction in model weight at approximately 22% over the past 30 years! People striving for "perfect" or "ideal" beauty logically mimic the ideal set by models, which today is thin. The health of people attempting to mimic this thin beauty ideal is put in serious jeopardy, especially if poor nutrition is combined with reduced caloric intake. These people suffer from never enjoying a meal and occasional overindulgence associated with great tasting food. These people pursuing the thin beauty ideal have, in essence, traded indulgence and eating enjoyment for the "thin" beauty ideal, based totally on a standard set by someone other than themselves. What a shallow (and less than enjoyable) existence!

2. Can't let their "hair down" or enjoy earthy adventures

Ever hear someone say, "I can't do that because I'll break a nail or mess up my hair?" People who have to look "just right" every minute of the day also trade adventure and fun for the "look" of beauty. Almost like a vase on a pedestal in a curio cabinet, these people are nice to look at but not very useful or practical. They are "dressed to kill", "always done up", never seen in casual/worn clothes, and wouldn't be "caught dead" doing "earthly" activities such as gardening, weeding, painting, hiking, etc.. These people are so image-conscious that they give up a big part of life's adventures and activities, activities which are deemed image-detracting. Women of this nature are typically called "useless", "dolls", "pampered pets", and "daddy's girls" among other names. Men are often called "snobs", "hoity-toity", or "pansies." These people often live their lives "from a glass case", unable to enjoy the adventures of people who are not afraid to get "down and dirty" and not fearful of temporarily blemishing their beauty or "image."

3. Flashy possessions

Ever know anybody who either wore fancy or very expensive clothes, or drove a flashy sports car, someone whom you thought was a really shallow person? Braggart, pompous, conceited, and self-centered are all words that come to mind to describe such flashy or "glitzy" people I've met before. These people tend to gravitate toward the flashy or "showy" side of beauty as a short-cut to being accepted or considered attractive. What these people tend to ignore is the shallowness of their actions and unnatural or "cosmetic" nature of the image they portray. They tend to place great value in their material possessions (i.e. clothes, car, home/apartment interior, office furnishings, etc.) in an attempt to be noticed or attract attention. The root of their beauty or attractiveness is these shiny self-extensions. Since they seem to lack the intestinal fortitude to work-out, reduce weight, or engage in other time-intensive image enhancing activity, they add the flashy accessories to "portray" beauty. These people are quite often considered as people not to be trusted, avoided, or are met with limited interaction (except for others who are flashy and shallow and share similar beauty values). They are often "pinnacles" of beauty in their eyes only, primarily attracting others of shallow and flashy nature. Many of these people lead lonely, shallow existences and often never fully understand what is uncommon about their approach to beauty and attractiveness.

4. Lack of satisfaction dating/nobody good enough

Ever know anyone who was very beautiful and could never find anybody to their liking. Ever know anybody who seemed really "picky" in terms of a potential dating partner's appearance? These people are so "caught up" in their own appearance and work so hard to achieve "beauty", they are unlikely to let just any slightly overweight, slightly blemished, or slightly balding, person date them! The beauty ideal that they worked so hard for was very clear in their mind—the weight, the look, the body tone, etc.. Their ideal partner is likely to also be very clear in their minds and must have exactly "the right look" to match their mental image. These (picky) people gravitate to "the right look" and often ignore the underlying character of the person behind the look. They continually make dating and mating decisions based almost solely on these external and extremely stringent appearance guidelines. The downfalls for these type of persons are:

a) Not satisfied with average or less than perfect (appearing) dating partners—severely limits the available choices.
b) Often selects the wrong date/mate due to reliance on transitory appearance standards. Ignores or overlooks more important compatibility factors such as morals, personality, character ("just as long as she/he looks nice").
c) May be very lonely due to the ivory appearance "tower" they create for themselves. "Nobody is good enough" or, "I can't seem to find the right person." (appearance-driven)
d) Are less than tolerant, even rude, to others who have not worked as hard as they have in attaining "the look."
e) May be considered stuck up, conceited, shallow, and to be avoided by persons of greater moral fiber.

5. Surrounded by shallow friends

People tend to make friends with people who are like themselves. People who are beauty-obsessed tend to surround themselves with other beauty-conscious people. Friends of people who are driven exclusively by appearance risk that these "friends" tend to be less than reliable and are often in the friendship as "takers", rather than "givers" or "equals." Appearance-driven people tend to enter in a friendship for some sort of personal gain and generally plan on giving nothing in return. Once the essence of personal gain is removed from the relationship, the relationship is no more! Just as with Mary and Mike, shallow, appearance-driven friends are transitory, and around primarily for the glitter and attention that surrounds other attractive people. They tend to thrive on knowing, and being seen with, the most attractive people (they can find). Their motivation is to be seen with the "in crowd" or "most attractive crowd", since these people define their own happiness by how they are seen and viewed by society. I have spoken with countless people who have known somebody who felt more attractive or important when among attractive people. In a sort of twisted beauty or value by association, people seem to feel a greater sense of self-value when seen with attractive persons. These people rely on external gratification and "basking" in the beauty of others to define their own gratification. They are actually just among the many appearance-driven "lost souls!"

CHAPTER 8 SUMMARY

A. Most people are of average appearance, unlike the models we see disproportionately in various media.
B. The beauty ideal has changed radically over the past 100 years.
C. Following the turn of the century, the trend for models and the beauty ideal has been toward thinner and leaner.
D. Some people define their happiness by how well they fit the beauty ideal set by the media and cosmetic producing companies.
E. The number of magazines, papers, and advertising associated with beauty has increased dramatically in the past 20-30 years.
F. Advertising, via an array of sources, disproportionately favors and highlights attractive people over unattractive people.
G. Beauty pleases, therefore beauty sells.
H. Many unattractive people have achieved great things in life.
I. Achievement comes from relying on an array of skills and maintaining the internal strength to believe in yourself more than your appearance.
J. Externally motivated persons rely on gratification from others for motivation. Those who are externally motivated tend to rely on, and be concerned with, appearances.
K. Internally motivated persons rely on gratification from within (themselves). Those who are internally motivated tend to rely on, and be concerned with, doing what they feel is right, regardless of any outside (external) criticisms or rejections.
L. Thomas Edison is an example of an internally motivated person who succeeded despite great criticism.
M. Eating disorders are at an all time high due to the concern with appearance and ever thinner beauty "ideal."

N.   The concept of "beauty at all costs" comes at a terrible price to persons who pursue this course of fulfillment.

O.   People obsessed with beauty are often lonely, shallow, and without friends and relationships of substance.

P.   People obsessed with beauty are also often at risk of experiencing eating disorders, known as "flashy" or unable to "let their hair down" and have fun participating in activities which detract from their appearance.

Q.   There is an advantage to being less than perfect or average in appearance and it may actually be enviable to being "beautiful at all costs!"

BIBLIOGRAPHY

American Economic Review, "Beauty and the Labor Market", 12/94, by Daniel Hamermesh and Jeff E. Biddle. With permission from by Daniel Hamermesh at University of Texas at Austin.

American Journal of Orthodontics, 60, pp. 175-183, 1971. "Facial Harmony", by N. Cox and F. Van der Linden. With permission from the Mosby-Year Book.

American Sociological Review, 90, 44-51, 1961. "cultural uniformity in reaction to physical disabilities", by Tom cash and Tom Pruzinsky, based on research of Richardson, Goodman, Hastorf, and Dornbusch. With Permission from the American Psychological Association.

Applied Cognitive Psychology (previously Human Learning), vol. 5, pp. 203-208, 1986. "The effects of facial disfigurement on social interaction", by N. Rumsey and R. Bull. Reprinted by permission of John Wiley & Sons, Ltd..

Behavior Therapy, 10, pp. 336-346, 1979. "Selection of heterosocial skills, II: Experimental validity", by T. Kupke, K. Calhoun, and S. Hobbs. With permission by the Association for the Advancement of Behavior Therapy, New York, NY.

Body Images, pages 63, 200, & 287, 1990, The Guilford Press, New York, NY.

Boston Globe Newspaper Company/Washington Post Writers Group. America's Sexual Myths, by Ellen Goodman, 10/13/94, Reprinted with Permission.

Canadian Journal of Behavioural Science, Vol. 3, pp. 377-387, 1971. "Communicator Attractiveness and opinion change", by Mark Snyder and Myron Rothbart. With permission by the Canadian Psychological Association.

Child Development, 37, pp. 519-532, 1966. "Infants' differential reactions to familiar and distorted faces", by J. Kagan, B. Henker, A. Hen-Tov, J. Levine, and M. Lewis. With permission by the Society for Research in Child Development.

Child Development, 55, pp. 267-276, 1984. "Abstract perceptual information for age level: A risk factor for maltreatment?", by V. McCabe. . With permission by the Society for Research in Child Development.

Child Development, 55, pp. 576-585, 1984. "Baby Beautiful: Adult attributions of infant competence as a function of infant attractiveness", by C. Stephan and J. Langois. . With permission by the Society for Research in Child Development.

The Guardian, March 24th, 1982. Based on an article by A. Kemp. Permission by Anthony Shoemaker, Permissions department, Wright State University.

Infant Behavior and Development, 2, pp. 329-339, 1979. "Facial feature determinants of perceived infant attractiveness", by K. Hildebandt and H. Fitzgerald. With permission from The Ablex Publishing Company.

International Journal of Cosmetic Science, vol. 2, pp. 77-101, 1980. "Cosmetics considered in the context of physical attractiveness", by J. Graham and A. Jouhar. With permission from Rapid Science Publishers, Philadelphia, PA.

International Journal of Cosmetic Science, vol. 3, pp. 199-210, 1981. "The effects of cosmetics on personal perception", by J. Graham and A. Jouhar. With permission from Rapid Science Publishers, Philadelphia, PA.

Journal of the American Optometric Association, "Anxiety induced by contact lenses and framed spectacles", by Drs. R.L. Terry, A.B., M.S., Ph.D. and D.J. Zimmerman, A.B., vol. 41, pp. 257-259, March 1970. With permission from the American Optometric Association.

Journal of Applied Psychology, 62, pp. 301-310, 1977. "Sexism and beautyism is personnel consultant decision making", by Tom Cash and B. Gillen. With permission from the American Optometric Association.

Journal of Consulting and Clinical Psychology (previously Journal of Consulting Psychology), 17, pp. 343-347, 1953. "The appraisal of Body-cathexis: Body cathexis and the self ", by Secord & Jourard. With permission from the American Psychological Association.

Journal of Educations Psychology, 67, pp. 599-609, 1975. "Effects of children's physical attractiveness on teacher's evaluations", by J. Rich. With permission from the American Psychological Association.

Bibliography

Journal of Experimental Social Psychology, 5, pp. 93-100, 1969. "Liking for an evaluator as a function of her physical attractiveness and a nature of the evaluation", by H. Sigall and E. Aronson. With permission by the Academic Press, Orlando, Florida.

Journal of Personality and Social Psychology, 24, pp. 285-290, 1972. "What is beautiful is good", by K. Dion, E. Berscheid, and E. Walster. With Permission by the American Psychological Association.

Journal of Personality and Social Psychology, 31, pp. 245-253, 1972. "Physical attractiveness, social relations, and personality style", by D. Krebs and A. Adinolfi. With Permission by the American Psychological Association.

Journal of Personality and Social Psychology, 29, pp. 299-304, 1986. "Beauty is Talent: Task evaluation as a function of the performer's physical attractiveness", H. Sigall and D. Landy. With Permission by the American Psychological Association.

Journal of Personality and Social Psychology, 37, pp. 1387-1397, 1979. "Communicator physical attractiveness and persuasion", by S. Chaiken. With Permission by the American Psychological Association.

Journal of Personality and Social Psychology, 38, pp. 131-140, 1980. "Contrast effects and judgments of physical attractiveness: When beauty becomes a social problem", by D.T. Kenrick and S.E. Gutierres. With Permission by the American Psychological Association.

Journal of Personality and Social Psychology, 39, pp. 660-668, 1980. "Physical attractiveness and courtship progress", by G. White. With Permission by the American Psychological Association.

Journal of Social Issues, JSI vol. 32, No. 1, pp. 147-168, 1976. "Breakups Before Marriage: The End of 103 Affairs", by Charles T. Hill, Zick Rubin, and Letitia A. Peplau. With permission from The Society for the Psychology Study of Social Issues and Charles T. Hill.

Journal of Social Psychology, 18, pp. 127-148, 1943, "The effect upon judgments of personality traits of varying a single factor in a photograph" by G. Thorton. Permission granted by the Helen Dwight Reid Educational Foundation. Published by Heldref Publications, 1319 18th Street, N.W., Washington, D.C., 20036-1802. Copyright 1943.

Journal of Applied Psychology, 28, pp. 203-207, 1944, "The effect of wearing glasses upon judgments of personality traits of persons seen briefly", by G. Thorton. Permission granted by the Helen Dwight Reid Educational Foundation. Published by Heldref Publications, 1319 18th Street, N.W., Washington, D.C., 20036-1802. Copyright 1944.

Journal of Psychology, 99, pp. 155-161, 1978, "Perceived physical attractiveness in married partners of long and short duration", by R. Bailey and J. Price. Permission granted by the Helen Dwight Reid Educational Foundation. Published by Heldref Publications, 1319 18th Street, N.W., Washington, D.C., 20036-1802. Copyright 1978.

Journal of Psychology, 114, pp. 151-157, 1983, . Permission granted by the Helen Dwight Reid Educational Foundation. Published by Heldref Publications, 1319 18th Street, N.W., Washington, D.C., 20036-1802. Copyright 1978.

Journal of Personality Assessment, 44, pp. 624-629, 1980. "Physical attractiveness, romantic love and equity restoration in dating relationships", by J. Critelli and L. Waid. With permission from Lawrence Erlbaum Associates, Inc., Publishers.

Mass Communication Quarterly (previously Journalism Quarterly), 56, pp. 283-288, 1979. "TV beauty advertisements and the role expectations of adolescent female viewers", by A. Tan. With permission from Association for Education in Journalism and Mass Communication at the University of South Carolina.

The New England Journal of Medicine, 275, pp. 1172-1174, 1966. "Obesity it's possible side-effect on college acceptance", by J. Canning and J. Mayer. Excerpted from information published in The New England Journal of Medicine. Copyright 1982 by the Massachusetts Medical Society.

Perceptual and Motor Skills, 42, p. 918, 1976. "Components of facial attractiveness", by Roger L. Terry and Judy S. Davis. With permission from Dr. C.H. Ammons, Editor.

Perceptual and Motor Skills, 42, p. 562, 1976. "Effects of eye correctives on ratings of attractiveness", by Roger L. Terry and David L. Kroger. With permission from Dr. C.H. Ammons, Editor.

Perceptual and Motor Skills, 46, pp. 1328-1330, 1978. "Length of hair and beardedness as determinants of personality impressions", by S. Mark Pancer and James R. Meindl. With permission from Dr. C.H. Ammons, Editor.

APPEARANCE IS EVERYTHING

Personal Best Health Letter "Healthlines", vol. XIII, No. 3, March 1995. Reprinted with permission from the Scott Publishing Company, Inc., Edmonds, WA. 1-800-888-7853.

Personality & Social Psychology Bulletin, 8, pp. 748-751, 1982. "For Appearance's Sake: Public Self-Consciousness and Make-Up Use", by L. Miller and C. Cox. Reprinted by permission by Sage Publications.

Personality & Social Psychology Bulletin, 9, pp. 351-358, 1983. "Mirror, mirror on the Wall...Contrast effects and self-evaluations of physical attractiveness", by T.F. Cash, D.W. Cash, and J.W. Butters. Reprinted by permission by Sage Publications.

Plastic and Reconstructive Surgery, 39, pp. 387-396, 1967. "Psychologic screening of inmates requesting cosmetic operations: A preliminary report.", by R. Kurtzberg, M. Lewin, N. Cavior, and D. Lipton. With permission by Williams & Wilkins, Baltimore, MD..

Psychological Reports, 28, pp. 975-980, copyright (c) 1971. "Stereotypes of scalp and facial hair as measured by the semantic differential", by Samuel Roll and J.S. Verinis. With permission from Dr. C.H. Ammons, Editor.

Psychonomic Science, 23, pp. 126-127, 1971. "The influence of iris color and pupil size on experienced affect", by Q. Jones and I. Moyel. With permission by The Psychonmic Society Publications, Austin, Texas.

Sassy Magazine, pp. 62-63, 86, March 1995. "The beautiful are damned", by Alison. Excerpt reprinted by permission on Peterson Publishing, Inc., New York, NY.

Sex Roles, 17, pp. 31-47, 1987. "The consequences of being overweight: A controlled study of gender differences", by Stake & Laurer. With permission from Plenum Publishing, NY, NY.

Social Psychology of Facial Appearance, pp. 9-10, 19, 28-29, 31,42, 45, 65-66, 134, 152-153, 158, 160-162, 195, 224, 229-230, 257, 270, 274-279, 1988, Springer-Verlag, NY, York, NY.

Teen Magazine, February 1995, article names reprinted with permission by the Peterson Publishing Company, 6420 Wilshire Blvd., Los Angeles, CA 90048-5515

U.S. News and World Report, article by William F. Allman, July 19, 1993. Permission by U.S. News & World Report, Reader Services.

Woman's World Magazine, January 3 1995, "Your beautiful Baby", p. 32.